# HowExpert to Become a Country Singer-Songwriter

## 101 Lessons to Become a Country Singer-Songwriter from A to Z

## HowExpert with Caroline Watkins

**For more tips related to this topic, visit HowExpert.com/country.**

# Recommended Resources

- HowExpert.com – Quick 'How To' Guides on All Topics from A to Z by Everyday Experts.
- HowExpert.com/free – Free HowExpert Email Newsletter.
- HowExpert.com/books – HowExpert Books
- HowExpert.com/courses – HowExpert Courses
- HowExpert.com/clothing – HowExpert Clothing
- HowExpert.com/membership – HowExpert Membership Site
- HowExpert.com/affiliates – HowExpert Affiliate Program
- HowExpert.com/writers – Write About Your #1 Passion/Knowledge/Expertise & Become a HowExpert Author.
- HowExpert.com/resources – Additional HowExpert Recommended Resources
- YouTube.com/HowExpert – Subscribe to HowExpert YouTube.
- Instagram.com/HowExpert – Follow HowExpert on Instagram.
- Facebook.com/HowExpert – Follow HowExpert on Facebook.

# Publisher's Foreword

Dear HowExpert Reader,

HowExpert publishes quick 'how to' guides on all topics from A to Z by everyday experts.

At HowExpert, our mission is to discover, empower, and maximize talents of everyday people to ultimately make a positive impact in the world for all topics from A to Z...one everyday expert at a time!

All of our HowExpert guides are written by everyday people just like you and me who have a passion, knowledge, and expertise for a specific topic.

We take great pride in selecting everyday experts who have a passion, great writing skills, and knowledge about a topic that they love to be able to teach you about the topic you are also passionate about and eager to learn about.

We hope you get a lot of value from our HowExpert guides and it can make a positive impact in your life in some kind of way. All of our readers including you altogether help us continue living our mission of making a positive impact in the world for all spheres of influences from A to Z.

If you enjoyed one of our HowExpert guides, then please take a moment to send us your feedback from wherever you got this book.

Thank you and we wish you all the best in all aspects of life.

Sincerely,

BJ Min
Founder & Publisher of HowExpert
HowExpert.com

PS...If you are also interested in becoming a HowExpert author, then please visit our website at HowExpert.com/writers. Thank you & again, all the best!

# Table of Contents

# INTRODUCTION

So you've decided you want to be a country music singer-songwriter! Congratulations, you have come to the right place. Like any business, the country music business requires a lot of hard work. It requires a lot of passion and love for music in general, but more than anything, it requires hard work. What you're about to read will cover everything you could possibly need to know about what kinds of work you'll have to put in toward achieving your goals and dreams and becoming a successful country music artist. We'll cover everything from songwriting to record labels and everything in between. We'll also be breaking down some of my personal songs and explaining things such as lyrics and melody and how to properly structure a country song, as well as some creative tips to help you write the best country songs possible. Also, at the end of each chapter, you'll find an "Expert Q & A", where I'll answer personally some of the most common questions I get about the country music business. You're about to read 101 tips that will tell you everything you need to know about how to become a successful country singer-songwriter, so get ready! Let's get started.

# Chapter 1: The Story

## *Country music is built on stories.*

Country music was built on one thing: storytelling. In a country song, you can tell a whole book's worth of a story, in 3-4 minutes or less. So let's talk about stories. A story is where a country song begins.

### 1. *Start with a story.*

One of the most famous phrases in country music, coined by the Nashville Songwriters' Association International (NSAI), is, "It all begins with a song." But what does a song begin with? *A story.* The first step to writing any country song is to think of a story you want to tell, and then to tell it with your song. Songs are such a special way to tell stories, because every art form essentially does this – paintings tell stories, poems tell stories, dances tell stories. Songs do it too. And by becoming a country artist, you are gaining the power to tell your own story too.

### 2. *Tell your personal stories.*

We all have stories we tell about our lives – first dates, prom nights, game-winning catches, profound conversations with our grandparents. If it's worth telling, it's worth writing about! It can be a story that happened to you as a child or a story that happened yesterday. You can draw from literally any story you have ever lived through. Even if the story is too detailed or outlandish to tell in song form, you can still think about the incident and remember exactly how you were feeling in that moment. Drawing from a feeling is a great way to create a song.

### 3. *Tell your friends' stories.*

A common misconception about music in general is that you have to write only about things that have happened to you personally. This, however, is far from the truth – if your friend has a great story to tell but they aren't willing to write about it, why not write about it yourself? It can be something that has affected you personally through them, or a story of a failed relationship they had or a crazy night they had that you had nothing to do with whatsoever. Inspiration is everywhere. It could even just be one sentence they say that sparks an idea.

## Some days you write the song, some days you live it.

### 4. *If it comes down to staying home and writing or going out and having fun – go out!*

You don't gain *life experience* without going out and *experiencing life*. If you don't go out and try to experience the real world, you'll never have anything to write about. More than that, you'll never have anything to write about that people believe you actually know about. One of the ways my friends often convince me to go out with them is to say, "But if you don't come, what are you going to write about tomorrow?" Nine times out of ten, it works on me, and I always end up with a new story to tell and a new song idea. Have you ever noticed that so many country songs talk about beer? That's because the writers make sure to allow themselves to go out and have a good time. If you allow yourself to go out and "live the song", the song almost writes itself the next day, or the day you decide to write the story. Once again, even if you don't write a song about that exact night or memory, you can certainly write about the feeling you felt while you were making that memory.

## 5. <u>Say yes as often as possible.</u>

If someone invites you to a party, go. If someone invites you on a date, go. If someone asks you to dance, dance! The more you say yes to, the more you experience, and the more you experience, the more you have to write about. A "yes" is not just a yes to one experience – it's a "yes" to a memory, a good time, a fun story to tell your grandkids! The more stories you can experience, the bigger and more exciting of a life you will live, regardless of whether or not you get a song idea out of it. So say yes! As long as it's not a dangerous yes, say yes. You will never regret it.

# 6. _Travel as often as possible._

There is so much perspective to be gained from leaving town. There are a million country songs about small towns, and a lot of times, that's because the writer sees their town in a new light once they leave and come back. When you travel, don't just look for inspiration in the towns you visit, but look for inspiration in your own hometown when you get back. Peoplewatching and sight-seeing are great inspiration – think about people you meet while travelling, but even just people you see that fascinate or interest you. Think about them and their story, or what their story might be.

# _Inspiration is everywhere. (Yes, everywhere.)_

## 7. _Write what you see._

There is a very simple rule to writing country songs: write what you see. Country music is based more on concrete details than thoughts, feelings, and concepts, and these concrete details give your song color and personality. If you see something that sparks any kind of inspiration whatsoever (even if it's just a word you like), write it down. If you see something that is beautiful or funny or exciting or incredible, write it down. The key is, whatever you see, it is bound to hold something special if you look at it hard enough. So in order to see things, you have to really *see* things – not just look at them. You have to study them, pay attention to them, look at the details. If you see something but don't really *see* it, it means nothing. If you see something and really *see* it – study its details and intricacies and purpose – you can write something absolutely awesome about it.

## 8. *Watch TV.*

Yes, even reality TV. Even though it might not be actual "reality", they are technically "real" people, and they have stories that can be written about, so write about them! TV holds stories just like real life holds stories. You can be "on the job" at all times, as long as you have your creative brain "on" at all times and are paying attention to your surroundings, or in this case, what you're watching. Creative jobs are special like that, because you can be "working" even when you're watching TV or movies. In fact, some songwriters even watch certain TV shows for the sole purpose of looking for ideas when they're stuck with writer's block.

If you're looking for some country music idea shows, try watching anything on CMT, or any show that seems to have country/Southern characters. This is especially helpful if you're not as Southern and aren't quite as familiar with Southern culture, but still love country music and want to write songs. Consider watching these shows your "homework." Pretty fun homework, right?

## 9. _Watch Movies._

On the contrary to reality TV: they might not be real characters, but they have real feelings that real people feel. Study those feelings, and write about them! Also, it's fun to play a song live and tell the crowd you got the idea from a certain movie that they all know about and love. It will give you something in common with your audience, something they can talk to you about when they meet you.

## 10. _Listen to podcasts._

Podcasts are a relatively newly popular phenomenon, but they are absolutely FULL of wise perspectives and quotes. There are plenty of podcasts to choose from, so find a few podcasts you enjoy listening to and listen to them regularly. When you listen, take notes. When someone says something you resonate with, write it down, and when someone says something that sparks a song idea, pause the podcast altogether to think about and flesh out the song idea, at least a little bit. If you let an idea pass you by without thinking about it deeply enough, it might lose its energy, and you might never want to come back to it. So, when someone says something that sparks your songwriting brain, let it sink in before you continue listening. It's also great to just sit and listen to a podcast with a notebook handy, instead of having to look for one as soon as you hear something you like. It's a helpful practice, because it's similar to listening to a song: you want to paint a picture and a scenario for your listeners just like podcasts hosts want to do. So, you can study what they do and say to make you feel like you're living in a different place or time or story, and then try to incorporate that skill into your own music.

## 11. <u>*Read, read, read.*</u>

This might come as a shock, but here's some good news: watching TV and movies, listening to podcasts, and reading can all be considered working when it comes to being a songwriter. Although you might not be writing the song at that moment, you can be gathering ideas from the characters, their stories, their hometowns, and more. Always be on the lookout for things you could use in a song. Even if you just see a word or phrase that you like, try to think about it more deeply and see if/how you could turn it into a song. The key is to always be paying attention and on the lookout for things that could spark a song idea. Country songs are based on real life and real people's feelings, so reading autobiographies, memoirs, and self-help books are especially good for sparking good country song ideas.

## 12. <u>*Listen to other country songs.*</u>

In many businesses, other people in the same field are competition. This is absolutely not the case in the country music world. 1, Southern people/country musicians are naturally down-to-earth and friendly people, so competition is not normally a factor. And 2, country musicians are constantly listening to and supporting each other's music. This is so important – country musicians are always paying attention to and supporting each other. And this means they listen to each other! Even if you aren't listening to your peers in the up-and-coming country music industry, you can listen to other country music in general, meaning the old school music is included. Getting inspired by other music is so important, because without copying older songs, you can get inspired by things you like in those songs, such as certain instruments and certain production techniques. Regardless of whether you listen to friends' music or Hank Williams and Dolly Parton, it's very important to listen to other country music in order to fit the bill for a country music artist.

## 13. *Use websites such as "Idioms.com", and try using different plays on words.*

Title ideas don't grow on trees! If you're struggling for title or hook or general ideas, it's great to look at certain words and/or phrases in general in order to spark or even create an idea. Idioms.com is a great place to start – the site constantly updates with different phrases and commonly used sayings, and in country music, using a common saying is a great way to start a catchy song. There are so many country songs that incorporate commonly used sayings as a play-on-words or just a way to make the song stick in the listeners' heads, so starting with certain idioms or phrases is a great place to get song ideas and start off an idea that is super strong and catchy. And spoiler alert, catchy is what makes you money!

Here are some prompts to get you into the mindset to write a creative country song, some prompts to make you think:

- What was the best night of my life?
- What did I feel like the night of my first kiss?
- What did I feel like the night of my first breakup?
- What do I see when I drive into my hometown?
- If I could say anything to my ex, I would say _____.
- If I could say anything to my significant other, I would say _____.
- What is the funniest thing that has ever happened to me?
- What would I say to my younger self?
- What would I say to my best friend if he/she was going through a breakup?
- What did I need to hear the last time I was heartbroken?
- What did the scene of my last breakup look like?
- What does heartbreak look like, without using the word "heartbreak" at all?
- Write a song without using the word "I" at all.
- Write a song that consists of entirely questions.
- Write a song with a person's name as the title.

- Write a song with a state's name as the title.
- Open a magazine and write a song based on the first word or headline you see.

Another thing that is very common and well received is a play on words. This means you use a phrase that can mean two different things and use it as the first meaning in the first part of the song, and then flip the meaning. Try thinking of a common, every day saying, and try to see if there's a way you can flip it to mean something else that you wouldn't normally expect. You usually use the phrase in its original way in the verses, and then flip the meaning usually in the hook of the song. The "hook" is either the line containing the title or the line leading up to the title, and then the title. Below, I'll show you a song I wrote that incorporates a play on words, and I'll break it down and explain what I did and how I did it.

**Can't Go Nowhere**

Caroline Watkins
7/20/18
VERSE 1
His mama works at the place
where I get my hair done
I pass his dad's shop
when I go for a run
His brother owns my favorite restaurant in town
And his best friend lives 2 houses down
Oh, I swear

I can't go nowhere

*[In this half-verse, I introduced the hook, but didn't give away the play on words yet. It's common in country music to introduce the hook at the end or beginning of each verse by just using a part of it, but not explaining what the play on words is. In this case, the hook I introduce is "I can't go nowhere." In this case, it means the singer cannot go anywhere physically, because if she does, she will run into her ex or someone he knows and she will have to talk about him or be reminded of him – which obviously, none of us want when going through a breakup.]*

It doesn't matter where I am
I always end up
Running into him
Or seeing his truck
Sitting at a stoplight or out with my friends
I'm doing all right and then he walks in
It ain't fair
I can't go nowhere

*[This is the second half of the verse, where I dive a little deeper into the hook. It's almost a way of tricking the listener into thinking the whole song will be about physical places the singer cannot go for fear of physically running into her ex. That's the best part about a play on words and then flipping it in the hook: the listener doesn't usually see it coming, and when it happens in the hook, it makes them go, "Ahh, I see what they did there!" This is the mark of a powerful hook, and that's the reason there's usually a musical break between the end of the chorus and the second verse, so that the hook and chorus can really*

*sink in in the listener's brain and let them see that the song is well-crafted.]*

CHORUS
Because everywhere I go
I'm reminded he's not mine to hold
So I just stand still like I'm frozen in time
Replaying the moment he told me goodbye
He's having the time of his life
moving on out there
But I can't go nowhere

*[And this is where the song flips. When the hook says, "He's having the time of his life moving on out there, but I can't go nowhere," that means she metaphorically cannot go anywhere. It flips from the physical meaning of the phrase to the metaphorical one. It means she cannot move on from this person, she is just stuck in this state of missing him, while he's out there moving on and leaps and bounds ahead of her in the moving on process. This hook makes the song even more sad – which is a good thing in country songs – because it means she cannot go anywhere, physically or metaphorically. It means this person has broken her heart so badly that she is literally stuck in one place.]*

VERSE 2
Every time I wake up
or I close my eyes
All I can see is my driveway that night
When his car is gone I just stare at my shoes
Tell myself to walk away, but all I can do
is stand there
Oh, I can't go nowhere

*[This verse takes on a slightly new meaning to the phrase – it means she is back in time at the night of their breakup. It means she is reflecting back on the night when her ex left her, and when he drove away, she knew she should either chase him or go back inside and start trying to get over him, but she was so blindsided and heartbroken that she just shut down. It means all she could do was just stand in the middle of the driveway and let what just happened sink in, which is a very sad image and lets the listener really put themselves in her shoes. In country songs, if you're using a play on words, it's best to try and use it in as many ways as possible, with as many different meanings as you can possibly come up with.]*

CHORUS
Because everywhere I go
I'm reminded he's not mine to hold
So I just stand still like I'm frozen in time
Replaying the moment he told me goodbye
He's having the time of his life
moving on out there
But I can't go nowhere

BRIDGE
I can't move, and I know I should
But where would I go if I could?

*[Ahh, the bridge – the part of the song that really brings it home and adds one more even more sad note to an already sad song. This bridge solidifies the fact that the singer is truly lost without her ex. She wants to move on, but she can't, because she was so dependent on this other person that she doesn't know where to go if she can't go to him. It's a very real*

*feeling that many of us experience in breakups, so it's important to try and say these hard feelings, because listeners can relate. She is asking herself this question with a little bit of hope, saying she knows she should move on, but she is still lamenting the fact that she just feels stuck and lost without him.]*

CHORUS
Because everywhere I go
I'm reminded he's not mine to hold
So I just stand still like I'm frozen in time
Replaying the moment he told me goodbye
He's having the time of his life
moving on out there
But I can't go nowhere

## *Expert Q & A*

**Q:** What's your favorite way to get songwriting inspiration?

**A:** Personally, I love to travel. It's nothing crazy, but if I start to feel like I'm running out of ideas, the best way for me to gather some new ideas is to just go visit family in another city or even just go for a long drive. I pay attention to the towns I pass through and think about the stories the people living there might be living, and I also love to spend time with the family I visit and try to gain some ideas from their stories.

The thing is, though, I'm not purposefully gathering song ideas when I'm travelling or talking to people, I'm just living and doing what I would normally do if I wasn't even a songwriter. Then, when I get back home, I find some quiet time to sit on my porch or alone with my thoughts and my guitar and reflect on everything I have seen and heard throughout my most recent travels. That's kind of the formula for my songwriting, and most songwriting, I suppose: have an experience, reflect on it, write about it, repeat. I know I've already said this, but living your life and not closing yourself off is so important in order to write good country songs. Because good country songs are about real life.

# Chapter 2: The Words

## *Choose your words wisely.*

Some people think the melody is most important, and some people think the words are. The answer is that both are equally as important, so neither can fall by the wayside. Each songwriter has a different writing process – some come up with the words first and some come up with the melody first, and neither process is wrong. We're going to start with the words.

### *14.  Words are powerful.*

Words are powerful – did you know that? Words have the power to either make or break someone's day, to make their day or break their heart, to make them laugh or make them cry or make them dance or make them fall asleep. Words have so much power than you would think. This means that every word counts when it comes to writing songs. In a lot of other genres, words don't mean quite as much, and they can fly right by without anyone noticing what they said or meant. In country music, though, the words mean everything. The words, arguably, carry the weight of the song, so if the words are weak, the song is weak. In order to write a song that is strong, you have to write a song with strong words. In other genres, one extra word flies under the radar. In country music, listeners tend to hang on every word, so one extra or one less word can really stick out. Pay attention to each and every word you use, and don't be afraid to edit and then edit again. Your words, each and every one, matter more than you know.

## 15.  *Every word matters.*

This means EVERY word – including an "and", a "but", a "'cause". These words don't seem to mean much while reading them, but in conversation, they add or take away a lot. And country music is SO based on conversation and conversational tendencies. A country song should sound like you took an everyday conversation you had with a friend and put it to music, and also tried to make the ends of the phrases rhyme. But aside from the melody and rhyme, it should feel effortless, and not forced in the least. So every word counts! Even if it doesn't seem like it, it does. So put it in, or keep it out, but whichever you do… think about it. Because it matters, more than you know.

## 16.  *Don't leave one word out or put one extra word in.*

One of my favorite cowriters prays before every session, "May we not leave one word out or put one extra word in." That means every single word counts! This means that one extra word can mess up the song and one less word can leave the song feeling slightly empty. If you use too many words, it can make it difficult for the listener to want to sing along and be able to remember the song. If you don't use enough words, the listener will not be able to get the full idea of the song, and you most likely won't be able to say everything you want to say in the song. So each and every word is important.

## 17. *Use creative words.*

Use a thesaurus! Think a little harder! Ask your friends! Don't use words that feel overused. Because words matter, they should be exciting, special, and meaningful. They should be unique – words that spark excitement in listeners. Every time you use a word that feels a bit boring or like it could be better, consider some alternate words. Consider words that are similar but might be a bit better, a bit more exciting, a bit more colorful. Changing just a few words can bring a song from average to great, from great to awesome.

## 18. *Don't use overly creative words.*

Although you should use creative words, you shouldn't use words that are overly creative. If you use a word that is outlandish and too creative, it will stand out too much and take away from the rest of the song. There is a fine line between creative and too creative, and usually, by reading the lyrics back in reading form and not in song form, you can tell whether it feels natural or not. Because country music is all about conversational lyrics, you should use words that are used in common conversation.

Using words that are too unique or different and wouldn't be used in a somewhat normal conversation will make your song like you're trying too hard. And country music listeners like to listen to songs that sound laidback and normal – not like they're trying too hard.

## 19. _Avoid words that are overused (i.e. love, hate, broken heart, apart)_

There are words that are overused in and across all genres. Even the average listener can list a few words that are overused and that they have heard too often to still appreciate. In earlier days of music, there hadn't been much said in songs before, so songwriters and singers had more freedom to sing words that come across as average now. And the reason they come across as average-sounding now is that they have been used to many times before. This is unfortunate because it makes our job harder, but it is also exciting, because it not only gives us a challenge, but it also gives us the ability to explore more words and word combinations that are more creative than we would settle for normally. In addition, you shouldn't just avoid these normal/slightly overused words in your songs in general, but especially in your titles. Your title should be something unique, different, and special – something that makes listeners see the title and ask themselves, "What is that about? I want to hear it and find out!" So if you must use some basic and overused words in your song, try hard not to use them in your title.

Here are a few of these words that you should try to steer away from as a writer, unless you have a unique spin on them. Included are a few word combinations/phrases that have been used as titles many times that you should try to steer away from as well. You will notice, they all have a lot in common: they have to do with love and relationships.

- Love
- Hate
- Break
- Broken
- Heart
- Apart
- Me and you
- You and me
- I love you
- I miss you

## 20. *Don't be afraid of a thesaurus.*

A thesaurus can help. A thesaurus can give you an exciting word in exchange for a boring word. If you have a boring word that feels like it fits your song's missing piece but just isn't the exact right word, use a thesaurus. It will help! It's never a bad thing to use a tool that can help you. It's not "cheating" – that's what things like a thesaurus are meant to be used for.

# *Words to a songwriter are like paint colors to a painter.*

## 21. *The right words give your song "color."*

In regards to color, country music is way more focused on this than other genres. Many other genres focus on ideas and feelings, on general concepts and overall moods. However, country music, as we have discussed, focuses on stories. And stories include many different colors. "Colors" is essentially a metaphor for "details" – if the story doesn't have details, you cannot fully see the story. If you choose the right words, you can fully paint the picture of your story. Picture the structure of the song (verse, chorus, verse, chorus, bridge, chorus) as the black lines on a coloring book page, and every word you get to fill in is a color. You can add any colors you want – the more colorful the better. But if it's all black and white, the excitement just isn't there. Even if it's a sad song, you can use blues and dark greys and dark greens and even some black. You can still use color for a sad song! Happy songs, you can obviously use more vibrant colors, or more vibrant words. The key is to add "colors" that fit your song and the feeling you are trying to portray with the song.

## 22. The goal of a country songwriter is to paint a certain picture or set a certain scene.

When you are creating a song, you should think about a few things: the story you are telling, the feelings and people you are describing, and the scene you are setting. In order to create a full and complete song, you need all of these things. And the scene is what makes the listener really feel like they are living inside the story you are trying to tell. Try to use sensory details in order to describe a certain scene. What did you hear? What did you taste? What did you smell? What did you see? What did you feel? All of these are important, and if you can do it naturally, it's great when you can include all of them. Try your best, but if you can't do it naturally (without being obvious that you are trying to include the five senses), at least include a couple.

## 23. Details, details, details.

If you think it's too detailed to put in a song, it most definitely is not. The more details, the better – if it's a unique detail, people will remember it. And that's what we want! When you are describing something, a story or a scene or something that happened, try to think of things about it that most people wouldn't notice. Below is a song of mine that you can reference for some slightly random details that paint a picture of a place that would otherwise seem simple and almost boring.

\*As a side note, I'll be using my own personal songs as examples and breaking them down – I would use some examples of other people's songs as well, but I don't have the rights to their songs, so I'll be using my own.

**Nothing to See Here**

Jason Massey/Caroline Watkins

7/24/18
If you ain't lookin for it,
you might miss that exit sign
First thing you'll see is that motel
Where no one stays the night
Next you'll pass that old BP
where the teenagers use fake IDs for beer
Ain't nothing to see here

Then there's the Sonic parking lot
And once you turn down main
There's a beauty shop and a Baptist church
A courthouse and a bank
It's like any other nowhere town
No keychains, coffee mugs or souvenirs
Nothing to see here

CHORUS
Nothing to see here
Unless you pack up and leave here
In Daddy's hand me down hatchback Chevy
Rear view torn off and ready
One day you come back
And everything you drive past

Makes you wonder why you swore for all those years
That there was nothing to see here

And that little screen door restaurant
is where I worked my first job
And I got my heart broken in that high school parking
lot
And that cliff out over Jasper Lake is where I had my
first drink
And faced my fears

CHORUS
Nothing to see here
Unless you pack up and leave here
In Daddy's hand me down hatchback Chevy
Rear view torn off and ready
One day you come back
And everything you drive past
Makes you wonder why you swore for all those years
That there was nothing to see here

It won't look like much to you
If you're only passing through

CHORUS
Nothing to see here
Unless you pack up and leave here
In Daddy's hand me down hatchback Chevy
Rear view torn off and ready
One day you come back
And everything you drive past
Makes you wonder why you swore for all those years
That there was nothing to see here

Here is another song I wrote that has lots of colorful details, including some snippets from actual conversations that I included in the song. Another thing I included in this song is a slightly different last chorus. It's common in country songs to change one or two lines in the last chorus – just in case there are one or two more things you feel like you haven't said yet.

## Drunk Girls in Bathrooms

Caroline Watkins
11.10.17

It's a universal place
Where everything is safe
Doesn't matter the city
Or the state you're in
It's a go-to destination
For women of all ages
Where everybody's instantly
Your new best friend

Just a couple stalls, a mirror, and a sink
But it's a little underrated, don't ya think?

CHORUS
Because it's
Girl, you don't need him
Here's a paper towel for the tears
You fix your makeup
I'll hold your beer
You got the best hair ever
And where'd you get those shoes

It doesn't matter who you are
or what you're going through
So wouldn't the world be nice
If we were all more like
Drunk girls in bathrooms

They don't teach you about it in school
It's just an unspoken rule
That if you don't know where to go
It's just the place to be
When you're ex is blowing up your phone
Or some creep won't leave you alone
It's a way out, it's an escape route
It's group therapy

CHORUS
Because it's
Girl, you don't need him
Here's a paper towel for the tears
You fix your makeup
I'll hold your beer
You got the best hair ever
And where'd you get those shoes
It doesn't matter who you are
or what you're going through
So wouldn't the world be nice
If we were all more like
Drunk girls in bathrooms

In a world where everybody's tearing everybody else
down
Lord knows, we can't let each other sit alone
On the cold tile ground

LAST CHORUS
So girl, you don't need him

Come on, dry your tears
And here's to us, 'cause we could all use
another beer
Let's go back out there
My friend, I got you
Gentlemen, take our word for it
Ladies, you know it's true
That the world would be nice
If we were all more like
Drunk girls in bathrooms

## 24.  *Show, don't tell.*

My favorite English teacher of all time used to always
tell us while writing, "Show the reader, don't tell
them." This applies to songwriting 100% and
especially in country music. You don't want to force
the listener to feel a certain way. You want to show
them the story, show them what happened, set the
scene, and then allow them to feel how they want,
without you forcing them. For instance, instead of
saying, "I was so sad," you could say, "I was shattered
like glass" – a more descriptive and colorful way of
describing the feeling of being sad instead of just
simply stating that you were or are sad. There are
plenty of ways to do this – simply, to start, avoid
saying, "I felt," or, "I was _____". Instead, say
something more descriptive, something that paints a
more descriptive picture. What kind of sad were you?
Were you sobbing on the couch? Were you cursing
and wanting to slash your ex's tires? Were you drunk
and wanting to call them? Ask yourself these
questions when you want to say a certain feeling, and

then, answer the question in the song. Chances are, if you've had the questions, your listeners will have them too. Get ahead of them, and answer the questions.

## 25. _Make the listener feel like they are watching a movie._

When you're writing a song, try and picture what the music video might look like. If it looks like it would be a boring music video, it might be time to reassess, because that most likely means the song will turn out to be boring. However, if you add a lot of details and color, that leaves room for tons of creativity and color in a music video. A great way to decide whether or not your song feels colorful enough is to close your eyes and listen back to the song while trying to decide whether or not you feel like you are in a different scene, standing in the middle of the story you are trying to tell your listeners. If you can feel that way when you listen to it, your listeners can. If you can listen to the song and feel like you are transported to a certain place, story, or moment, you have done a good job.

# *Rhyme, rhyme, rhyme!*

## 26.   *Rhyme is what makes your song catchy.*

If you want to write a song that is memorable and fits the guidelines of a classic country song, you need a song that fits a classic country rhyme scheme. There are many different rhyme schemes, and all of them work! They can have different rhyme schemes from verse to chorus, but the key is, they have to have some sort of rhyme scheme, or they won't stick easily in the listeners' brains. If a song doesn't have a rhyme scheme, it is immediately less easy to remember. Our brains are not trained to remember full monologues in one listen, but if your song has a distinct and easy to follow rhyme scheme, your listeners could know most of the words to your chorus by the third time they hear it. This is a great sign!

Below are 2 songs I wrote with classic country rhyme schemes in both the verses and the choruses, both different rhyme schemes. (If 2 lines have the same letter, that means they rhyme with each other.)

**I Got Time**

Alyssa Micaela/Caroline Watkins
4/9/20
    (A) I got time for letting go
    (A) Won't be this hard I know
    (A) Swear some nights it goes so slow

(A) But I got time for letting go

(B) I got wheels for moving on
(B) Full of sad songs
(B) An open road that takes me home
(B) I got wheels for moving on

CHORUS
(C) You used to be mine
(D) You used to love me too
(C) I used to think I'd never make it
(D) Getting over you
(E) But every day I'm getting better
(F) And I know I'll be fine
(G) Might take me a while
(F) But I got time

And another one, with a different rhyme scheme:

## Happy Hour

Rian Ball/Caroline Watkins
3/9/20

(A) I was just trying to get out of my house
(A) At least that's it's how it all started out
(B) Just gonna be a drink with you
(B) Nothing crazy nothin new
(A) Guess I had too much somehow

(C) I used to think we were the kind
(C) To hang around 'til closing time
(C) To shut it down, and burn it up all night

CHORUS
(D) But it was just Tito's with the soda
(E) Corona with a lime
(F) It was pitchers on the table
(E) Sun setting in your eyes
(F) Never a morning not hungover
(G) Or a night that wasn't fun
(H) We were 4 to 7, 2 for ones
(I) 'Til the day that we were through
(I) Aww, but it was just a happy hour to you

It was all just fun and games
Until I didn't wanna play
Thought you were just what I was looking for
But I was in it for a little more
Guess you didn't want the same

BRIDGE
I used to think we were the kind
To hang around 'til closing time
To shut it down, and burn it up all night

Notice, the first one has more rhymes than the second. More classic country songs tend to have more rhymes than modern country songs, whereas modern country songs have a few less rhymes. However, modern country songs have more internal rhymes, which means they rhyme inside certain phrases, but not always at the end of the phrase. Country songs rhyme in as many ways as possible – it makes them catchy, and it makes them easy to listen and sing along to. If listeners can't sing along, they usually don't want to hear it, and they definitely don't want to hear it in a live show.

## 27.   *If your song doesn't rhyme, listeners have a harder time remembering it.*

Think about songs that stick in your head. Do they rhyme, or do they have a lot of words that don't sound anything like each other? Think about the songs that you listen to and how similar the words are to each other, then try to mimic that. Think about songs that get stuck in your head, and try to focus on their rhyme schemes, and what about them makes the song get stuck in your head. Whatever works for those songs, try to make it work in your own song, without copying of course. You can draw inspiration without totally copying.

## 28.   *The more unique of a rhyme, the better.*

Unique = memorable. If your song is unique, listeners will remember it. And if your words are unique, your listeners will not only remember them, but the song in general! That means you have to consider not only unique words, but also, unique rhymes. This means rhymes are not only one word and another word, but one phrase with another phrase. Rhyming one phrase with another phrase is a great way to make your song not only memorable but also unique. Here are some examples of unique rhymes. And the good thing is, in country music, things are so conversational that it never, ever, EVER has to be an exact rhyme for it to work. If it's close enough, it is just as powerful.

- Miss you / Kiss you
- Celebration / participation
- Forget you / Regret you
- Remind / Rewind
- No more / For sure

These are just a few – the more creative the rhyme you can find, the better! The key is, if you can find a rhyme that is creative but still conversational and could be used in a normal dialogue, you have struck gold. So, use that one word and/or word combo, and stick to it! Try to think of words with multiple syllables that rhyme. The more syllables that rhyme, the stronger it feels (for instance, celebration and participation.) These are ways to really cement the words in your listeners' heads. And that's the goal!

## 29. *Rhyme websites are your friend.*

Many songwriters consider using a rhyme assistant website as a cop-out or a crutch. Some rely on their own brains to give them plenty of rhymes to use. However, rhyme websites are an incredible friend to songwriters, and there is no rule book anywhere that says using rhyme websites or books is a bad thing. It is not "cheating" on your writing in any way – it is helping! If you need help with a rhyme, use rhymezone.com or rhymebrain.com – or one of the many other websites that help specifically with rhymes. These website spice up songs and other writing pieces because they give you so many other options to choose from. But here's the thing – you never have to choose one of these rhymes! They are just very credible and helpful sources to adding more rhymes. Your brain should be occupied on coming up with creative thoughts and stories and ideas, and rhymes should be a secondary thing – therefore, using a rhyming website is perfectly acceptable and helpful on your song journey. Ultimately, whatever needs to be done to make your song memorable and enjoyable to listen to, you should do it. Fight for your song to be great, not just good.

## *EXPERT Q & A*

**Q:** What's your best advice for what to do when you get stuck and can't think of creative enough words?

**A:** My number one piece of advice, as you have probably noticed, is that country songs are conversational. So, if I get too hung up on trying to come up with creative words and rhymes, I will try to forget about the rhyme for a moment and think about what I would say if it didn't have to rhyme, if I could just say whatever I wanted as if I was having a conversation. I write that down, then, I try to think of ways I could make the ends of the phrases rhyme, by using a thesaurus to find words that mean the same thing. Obviously, sometimes you have to change a little more in order for the song to rhyme, but if you start with an actual conversational statement and work around that, it's very helpful in writing an altogether conversational and still catchy song.

# Chapter 3: The Music

And now, the second half of the song: the melody, or the music. The music is what gives the song a certain unspoken feeling. A melody, if constructed correctly, can leave a lasting mark on a listener's brain. And if a great melody is paired with great lyrics – well, that's what makes a great song. It needs both.

## *The melody sets the tone.*

### *30.    The melody is the second piece of the song that makes it catchy.*

A catchy melody is hard to teach, but it is best learned by listening to other melodies that are catchy to you. If you are listening to a song and it seems to get stuck in your head, make a note of it. Then, try to study it and decide that it is about the song – for these purposes, melody specifically – that makes it stay in your head. Is there one note that stays constant in every line throughout the whole song? Is there one note that is held out longer in certain lines? Are there certain lines that go higher than others, but still stay in the same rhyme scheme? In most cases, a catchy melody does not differentiate too much from the verses to chorus. So, pay attention to songs you like and what they do, then draw inspiration from and try to do something similar to that. You should never copy another person's music, but you can certainly get inspired by what they do and try to understand what they do that

you like, and then try to do something similar – not
the same.

## 31.   _Learn to play an instrument._

When you learn to play an instrument, you are able to
create melodies much more easily. Playing an
instrument gives you a baseline for starting a melody
and then developing it and its details from there,
depending on how well you know how to play. When
you can play an instrument, you can use certain
chords to create the frame of a song, and then you can
build off that. If you can play an instrument at an
expert level, you can create the entire melody for a
song without any lyrics. This means if you add catchy
lyrics, your song will certainly be catchy altogether,
because a catchy melody and catchy lyrics create a
virally catchy song. All this said – if you can learn to
play an instrument, you will automatically be ahead of
the game. In country music, you should try to start
with either guitar or piano.

In addition, knowing how to play an instrument gives
you a new sense of power. It gives you more freedom
to create original songs, because you have a basis to
do it instead of pulling random melodies out of the
air. You can start with a few simple chords and build
an awesome melody just from those simple few. It
also gives you the ability to play live by yourself and
without having to pay a guitar player if you are just
playing acoustically. This is a very important skill and
will really show your musical abilities when playing
live if you can play the instrument yourself instead of

needing someone else to do it. Also, it will save you money because you will not have to pay as many people to play for you.

## 32.   *Learn to play an instrument well.*

Being able to play an instrument is one thing. Being able to play an instrument WELL is a whole other thing. If you want to become a star country singer-songwriter and you can play an instrument super well, you are leaps and bounds ahead of the game. When you are only playing an instrument for show, audiences can tell – as we've said, country music is all about authenticity. But if you are playing an instrument because you are truly skilled in playing it, you will not only feel more confident onstage, but also, your fans will be more confident in your pride in your music and melodies. When you can learn to play an instrument well, you can learn to come up with melodies that are unique and original, melodies that perfectly fit your song ideas and how they should be executed.

In addition, there is an even more heightened level of confidence that comes from being able to play an instrument well, versus just being able to play one at all. It gives you a sense of confidence and showmanship onstage that is visible to an audience and respected by your other bandmembers. It also makes you feel more comfortable onstage, simply because you can do more onstage. Overall, learning to play an instrument with skill is a serious and significant addition to your career in general.

## 33.  _Decide on a melody that fits with the lyrics._

Your melody and your lyrics are not 2 separate things
– they are cohesive and should perfectly get along
with each other. Your melody should represent your
lyrics, and vice versa. If your lyrics are sad, your
melody should feel sad, using slower chord changes
and beats per minute (BPM) and slower rhythm
altogether. Your chords should also me more minor
and sharp/flat in order to give off a sadder feeling. On
the other hand, if you want to convey a more positive
message with your song, you should use a higher BPM
and more major chords than minor chords in order to
match the melody and lyrics together. When they
match together, it is the perfect recipe for a catchy and
memorable song. There is also a certain level of "can't
put my finger on it" that makes a melody a lyric feel
right together. The only way to describe this is that
you'll know when it feels like. That means you have to
keep trying to get it right, as long as it takes, until it
feels right. You will definitely know when you know.

## The melody hooks the listener.

## 34.  _A catchy melody + catchy lyrics =_ _hit song._

If your melody is catchy and your lyrics are catchy,
you have a perfect recipe for a hit song. And if you
have worked hard to make the 2 coincide, you have
set up the perfect scene for a catchy song. However, it

can't just be a catchy melody and catchy lyrics: it must be catchy lyrics, a catchy melody, and a general relationship between the two, meaning the melody and lyrics must fit together properly. If they fit together and their melody and lyrics all work together, a hit song is born. You know your song is catchy when you find your own self singing it after writing it. If it doesn't get stuck in your own head, it definitely won't get stuck in your listeners' heads. So, that might mean it's time to go back and change some things to make it catchier.

## 35. *The first thing the listener hears is the melody.*

If you're more of a lyric writer than a melody writer, it's hard to accept, but the fact of the matter is that the melody is almost always the first thing that listeners hear. There is almost always at least 2 bars of solid instrumental before the lyrics start to be sung. It's a common saying in the music world that you have 5 seconds to catch the listener's attention, and as listeners ourselves, we all know this to be 100 percent true – if we hear a song that starts with a melody we don't like, we will immediately flip to the next song. The melody hooks the listener – the lyrics win them over. The melody starts the interest, the lyrics solidify it. Both are equally as important as far as carrying the weight of the song (a bad melody with good lyrics, or vice versa? No thank you!) But that being said, the melody is what has the opportunity to start it off strong. After all, first impressions are everything.

## 36. _If the melody is too complicated, listeners can't sing along._

Yes, it's tempting to show off your chops, to add in as many key changes as possible and leap from the bottom of your register to the top, and then the top to the bottom, and then throw in a few minor chords, and make it as different and shocking as possible. But here's the thing: there is a time and place for each of these unique techniques, but their time and place is not all in one song. If you want to show off something cool, choose that one thing for one song, and then add another thing in another song, and so on and so on. This creates balance. Country music listeners want to be able to sing along to your songs, and no one will sing along if they don't know all the notes or can't reach the notes even if they do know them. You don't necessarily have to make your song simple and basic, because this can get boring. However, simplicity is way underrated, because in the country music world, simple can be absolutely beautiful. If you listen to country radio right now, you will hear a lot of simplicity – a lot of short phrases with the notes drawn out, a lot less words than some other genres. This is a good thing! It makes the songs catchy and easy to get stuck in the listeners' heads. And remember, that's what we want: for the listeners to not be able to stop singing your song in their head, so naturally, they will listen to it. When trying to write a catchy song, it's not exactly the time to show off how wildly creative you can be with your leaps and jumps from note to note.

# Create your own unique melody.

## 37.  Don't steal from a song that has already been done.

Let's be honest – it's hard not to accidentally steal from a song that has already been done. There are SO many songs in the world, and it's hard to remember which melodies you have heard before and which you have created in your own head! Chances are, if you're writing a song and you say, "I feel like I've heard this melody before..." you probably have. That means you need to change your melody! You are perfectly capable of coming up with a melody that is unique and different and all your own, and if your listeners hear your melodies and think you copied them, they will respect you much less. (In addition, you will respect yourself much less.) So that means you have to think long and hard when you start a melody and comb your brain to make sure it isn't a melody you've heard before. If it's a melody you feel familiar with but can't put your finger on where you've heard it, it's best to be safe and change at least a few notes. You won't regret it!

## 38.  Copyright is a real thing.

It's very important to study and get familiar with copyright law. Copyright is a real thing: if you copy someone else's song, you can get in big trouble and get into a lawsuit that you don't have the money to pay for. Many famous musicians have gotten into this situation, including Taylor Swift, Kanye, and more. In the country music world, many of the same chords are used, and this is okay. However, if the same melody and the same lyrics are used in a combination, and in addition, if the same lyrics are used in succession, you can get sued for copyright. It also depends on reasonable means of access – meaning you can only sue someone for stealing your idea if they have a reasonable means of having accessed your song. However, if you are stealing someone else's idea, they will most likely try to sue you, because no one likes to have their ideas stolen! Study up on the rules of copyright law so that you can prevent a situation like this before it starts. When you know the copyright laws, you will be conscious of them every time you go into a session, and sometimes even overly conscious – which is totally okay, because it will encourage you to be even more creative than you normally would. You are a songwriter and artist, after all, so that's your job! You are a creative person, so you are capable of coming up with your own unique ideas. If you feel your melody is too similar to another person's, the answer is simple: change your melody. Again, it's better to be safe than sorry, and it's also better to be creative than to copy someone else!

## 39. _Use basic chords but unique melody._

There's a special secret that the country music world has figured out about creating unique melodies with basic chords. And here's the secret: use the same variation of chords, just in a different order. And in addition, you can create any vocal melody on top of this, as long as you keep the instrumental chords similar in each song. This is a surefire way to make your song catchy! Your listeners subconsciously hear the same chords in a slight variation and it strikes a metaphorical chord with them that they have heard something like this before, and it made them happy. This makes them automatically like the song, and automatically makes it stick in their head. This doesn't mean you have to limit yourself to these few chords, but ultimately, to decide which 5-6 chords you love to use, and to use them in most all of your songs, even if you change the vocal melody in other ways. You want your listeners to remember you, and in doing this, they will. In addition, you will create your own personal "sound", and that, as we have discussed, is super important.

## 40. *Follow the structure of ta song.*

The structure of a country song is SO important in creating a catchy, lasting country song. No matter how creative you are, if you want to create a song that sticks in listeners' minds and classifies as real country music, it's important to follow the structure of a song as best as possible. Listener's expect to hear the common structure of a song. You can wow them with the creative words you use and things you say, but if the right structure doesn't happen, the listeners can get thrown off and confused, which is the last thing you want.

So what is the structure of a song? The structure of a country song is typically: VERSE, CHORUS, VERSE, CHORUS, BRIDGE, CHORUS. It's okay to differentiate from this – sometimes, a country song will skip a bridge in exchange for a solo or instrumental part. Sometimes, a country song will add another verse after the last chorus. But for the most part, the above is the most common structure for a song. Below, you'll find a couple of my songs that have the general structure for a country song, separated into their individual parts. If you can follow this structure, you can certainly create a catchy, stand-out country song.

**Grocery Shopping**
Jimi Bell/Taylor Edwards/Caroline Watkins
6.14.18

**VERSE 1**
Right now, you're all about me
But soon, I'll be your flavor of the week
'Cause you take me out, then you don't call
Blame it on something, 'cause nothing's your fault
Guess your Mama didn't teach ya
Or maybe you just didn't listen

**CHORUS**
You can't pick it up, put it down
Check it out, turn around
Leave it for someone else to clean up
It ain't a 24/7, free ride to heaven
Walk in and get it whenever you want

Cashier counter, little small talking
Leave it on the shelf 'cause you found a better option
Sorry, love ain't grocery shopping

**VERSE 2**
I didn't see you holding her hand
But I got eyes in this town, yeah it's too small to hide
in
And all your strolling
Halfway down the aisles
It's gonna catch up to you
And I won't feel sorry for you

**CHORUS**
You can't pick it up, put it down
Check it out, turn around
Leave it for someone else to clean up
It ain't a 24/7, free ride to heaven
Walk in and get it whenever you want
Cashier counter, little small talking
Leave it on the shelf 'cause you found a better option
Sorry, love ain't grocery shopping

**BRIDGE**
So if you're looking for a sale
Baby, you can go to hell

**CHORUS**
You can't pick it up, put it down
Check it out, turn around
Leave it for someone else to clean up
It ain't a 24/7, free ride to heaven
Walk in and get it whenever you want
Cashier counter, little small talking
Leave it on the shelf 'cause you found a better option
Sorry, love ain't grocery shopping

Here's another one that skips the bridge, and uses a musical solo instead. Notice, there is a complete third verse instead of a bridge, and the last chorus has a couple lines that are different than the original chorus. This is a great way to add a bridge thought without adding an entire bridge.

## First Times Last

Tori Tullier & Caroline Watkins
4.9.18

**VERSE 1**
The first time
Your mama took you to the record store
Cash in your pocket 'cause you saved up for
Your very own Dixie Chicks CD
The first time
You got the behind the wheel, put the key in the ignition
Feeling so cool, just a kid on a mission
Your brother's hand-me-down Honda CRV
And never in your life had you felt so free

**CHORUS**
Something 'bout the way it feels
When you know it's gonna be a one time deal
The second and the third go out the window fast
No matter how hard you try
Never again is it gonna feel like
It did, so you thank God that
The first times last

**VERSE 2**

The first time
your best friend's parents went out of town
Took a bottle of Fireball and passed it around
That someone's older sister bought with her fake ID
The first time
he kissed you, on the basement couch
You tried to keep it together, but your heart's beating
out
of your chest
And in your head, you're swearing he's the one for me

**CHORUS**
Something 'bout the way it feels
When you know it's gonna be a one time deal
The second and the third go out the window fast
No matter how hard you try
Never again is it gonna feel like
It did, so you thank God that
The first times last

**VERSE 3**
The first time
You can't look at him from the passenger seat
And you know what's coming, but don't wanna believe
When he tells you he don't love you like he did
And you grow up and move on with your life
But you still hear his name every once in a while
And your heart can't help but go right back there
again

**LAST CHORUS**
Something 'bout the way it feels
When you know it's gonna be a one time deal
The second and the third go out the window fast
No matter how hard you try
Never again is it gonna feel like

It did, so you thank God that
The past is the past
The first times last


And lastly, here's one that does have a bridge,
but the bridge is actually a repeat of a line from the
first verse (rather, the pre-chorus). Notice, this one
has a few more words. When a song has more words,
it's generally a good idea to skip the bridge and use a
solo or to repeat an earlier line in order to give the
listener a bit of a break to let the words digest and
register with them. Then, when the last chorus hits,
they can appreciate it and resonate with it even more
than the first time they heard it.


**One In Every Town**
Jason Massey/Connie Harrington/Caroline Watkins
3/30/20

**VERSE 1**
There's a place with a red front door
Flowers on the porch
Like your mama's house
There's a truck at a Main street light
Looks just like
You driving around

It's a double take
Of a sun-tanned face
Or a laugh I hear in a crowd

**CHORUS**

There's one in every town
Every road I run down's
Got a little piece of us
No matter where I go
Or how hard I try
I can't leave 'em in the dust
There's a memory
One more you and me
Just keeps finding me somehow
There's one in every town

**VERSE 2**
There's a bar band playing our song
Girls singing along
But they ain't got a clue
I'm sitting here trying not to lose it
Trying to drink through it
But missing you

Hell, I could go
from the East to West Coast
But I'd still see a ghost or two

**CHORUS**
There's one in every town
Every road I run down's
Got a little piece of us
No matter where I go
Or how hard I try
I can't leave 'em in the dust
There's a memory
One more you and me
Just keeps finding me somehow
There's one in every town

**BRIDGE/REPEAT PRE-CHORUS**

It's a double take
Of a sun-tanned face
Or a laugh I hear in a crowd

**CHORUS**
There's one in every town
Every road I run down's
Got a little piece of us
No matter where I go
Or how hard I try
I can't leave 'em in the dust
There's a memory
One more you and me
Just keeps finding me somehow
There's one in every town

# *Expert Q & A:*

**Q:** What do you start with: the lyrics or the melody?

**A:** I think it depends on the day, and I also think it depends on the person. I actually have a lot of friends who only write lyrics, and that's the beauty of cowriting, because since I do lyrics and melody, I can write with a friend who only writes lyrics and I can just take the melody into my own hands. But ultimately, if you're a songwriter, I think the ideas will come to you in both lyric and melody form some days, in just melody form another, and in just lyric form another. There is no wrong way! For me, what usually comes first is the title, and then I will work around that. Usually, when I sit down to cowrite, we decide on a title and then try to find a melody that fits the title and the mood or message we are trying to convey. Then, we'll write the rest of the lyrics. However, some days, a couple lines come at a time, or a made-up melody gets stuck in your head – like I said, it really does depend on the day. The key is to take what you have and then build around it. Songwriting is really cool like that; you start with nothing and walk out with something that was never there before.

# Chapter 4: The Recording

Once your song is created, it's time to take the next step: you have to get your song recorded. You have to get your song into a recorded form that can be shared in ways other than live shows – streamed on Spotify and Apple Music and Pandora and other streaming platforms, in addition to being able to be sold on CDs and vinyl records. In order to get your song recorded, you have to find a producer.

What does a producer do exactly? Yes, it can get confusing, because there arc many different parts of your music career team, and we've all gotten them confused before. Your producer, however, is responsible for recording your song and bringing it to life. They record your vocals, as well as various instruments to back up your song and give it a full, complete feeling. Let's talk about producers, and how to get a recording that will make you stand out from the crowd.

## *Choose your producer wisely.*

### 41. *Choose a producer who understands what you want to sound like.*

Choosing the right producer for your music is SO important, and the first thing to look for in a producer is this: understanding. Your producer absolutely has to understand who you want to be as an artist and what you want to sound like. If they do not understand you or your view of your artistry, they will never be able to properly create the sound you want to hear, so you will constantly be struggling to make your vision clear to them. Therefore, you must find a producer who understands who you want to be and what you want to sound like, because that way, they will be able to bring your creative vision to life.

## 42. *Learn how to offer your producer direction.*

Unfortunately, your producer cannot hear what you are hearing in your head. There is no way for you to show them exactly what you're hearing in your own mind. (And if so, you would be producing your own music!) That means you have to learn how to offer your producer the right direction to help him or her produce the music you want to hear. You should look up certain production terms, such as ambience, reverb, EQ, and more – that way, you can tell them exactly what you want to hear, even if you can't execute it yourself. When you can speak to them in proper production terms, they can understand and translate what you want to hear into real music and bring your vision to life.

## 43. *Show your producer different artists' sounds you like to give them inspiration.*

Although you can't show your producer exactly what you're hearing in your head, you can show them what you like to hear when listening to other artists. Give them a list of artists you like and their production, or even other producers you like. Send them as many as possible! Also, don't just tell them the artists – tell them what you like about specific songs, and why you like those specific songs. For instance, point out that you like the drum sounds used, or you like the type of guitar, or you like the banjo being the focal point of the song. In addition, tell them what you don't like. By giving your producer a detailed list of what you want to hear and don't want to hear based on other, real, concrete examples, they can ultimately piece together all the various things you like to create something that fits what you are looking for.

## 44. *Make sure you get along with your producer.*

You're going to spend a lot of time with your producer. Late nights in the studio, phone calls about certain parts of the production you like and don't like, and often, even cowriting with them. So feeling comfortable and enjoying being around them is super important! If someone is a great producer but you can't stand to be around them, you should most definitely find a different producer. Because chances are, the feeling is mutual and they feel the same about you, which means they will not prioritize working on your projects, and this is never a good situation to get into. So make sure you are more than coworkers, but also, could even be friends.

## *A bad recording can ruin a good song.*

### 45. *If you end up with a bad recording, don't be afraid to redo it.*

If you have an awesome song but the production isn't good, you can absolutely ruin your perfectly good song. The production can overshadow your song, and that's all listeners will hear. Many things can ruin production: vocals being drowned out by instruments, instruments that don't fit the vibe of the song, or just an overall sound of unprofessionalism. If you get back a recording from a producer but you don't like it, don't be afraid to tell them you want to change it! If they give it another shot or they change it and you still don't love it, you should find a different producer. Ultimately, you might lose money paying for production, but you will make it back in the end when your song is a hit!

## 46.  _Your recording should add to your song, not take away from it._

If your recording doesn't make your song sound even better than it was before, it's not right. You should never feel like your song doesn't shine in an even brighter light when produced – it should just sound bigger, more enhanced, even better than how it sounds acoustically. If you listen to the recording and it makes your song sound worse or doesn't add anything to your song, have the courage to either redo it or find a new producer. It might take some more tome to redo it or find a new producer, but ultimately, it will pay off in the end. If you release a song you are not totally and fully proud of, you will most likely regret putting it out into the world. And obviously, you don't want this.

## 47.  _Look for a producer who has worked with artists you like. If you can't afford them, have them recommend someone._

A great way to know you will work well with a producer is if they have worked with an artist you like and you like their production as well. This means the producer will almost definitely be able to work with what you want to sound like. Sometimes, artists you like might be higher up in the industry, so their producers will charge more. If you can get in touch with these higher up producers, ask them if they could recommend anyone and could steer you to a producer that is more in your price range. Producers almost always have a young up-and-comer they support and would be glad to give them business by sending you in their direction.

## 48.   *You don't have to break the bank to record a country song. A simple, clean, guitar and/or piano-vocal will do.*

If you don't have a big budget for recordings, fear not! Getting a full-band, big demo can get a little costly, no matter who you use. But if you don't have the means to do this, you can absolutely get away with a simple, clean, guitar and/or piano recorded with your vocal. Sometimes, in fact, less is more, especially in country music. Sometimes, a clean guitar or piano-vocal sounds even better than a fully produced song, because it makes the song more organic and lets your talent really shine through without the possibility of distraction from production that is too intense. So don't worry if this is all you can afford, because sometimes, it's even better than doing a full band demo session!

If you really want to save money, you should invest in some very basic recording equipment for your own computer and record your basic demos on your own. That way, all you will have to pay for are a basic USB microphone or recording interface and some headphones, and then possibly one of the production softwares such as Logic or ProTools. However, if you really don't want to break the bank, you can usually get away with just using GarageBand on your Mac, as long as you make sure it is very simple and clean. Again, the simpler and cleaner the better, and if you can get the job done with just some cheap equipment and GarageBand – by all means, do it!

# *Don't use too many instruments.*

## 49. <u>When it comes to country music, the more real instruments, the better.</u>

Country music is real: real people, real stories, and real music. This applies to production too – country music is based on the use of real, not computerized instruments. And although they have their time and place, there's one thing you need to know about using real instruments in your production: the more real instruments you use, the more country you sound. The real instruments I'm talking about are acoustic guitar, electric guitar, mandolin, banjo, tambourine, a real drum kit, a fiddle, a piano, and more. Use real claps and snaps too! If you're going for a more pop-country feel, you can still incorporate a lot of real instruments and still add in some computerized ones.

## 50. <u>Sometimes, the less instruments, the better.</u>

Yes, we've said it already, but it's important: in country music, less is often more. If you have a ballad song, it's always great to use less instruments, because the less instruments, the less drowned out your vocal has the chance of sounding, and the lyrics can really sink in and allow the listener to really process and feel them.

## 51. *Start with a guitar or piano.*

A guitar or piano is the building block for your full song. Start with the chords on guitar or piano. These are the two instruments that are almost vital to every song you ever record, so they should be where you start. After you record a track of one or both of these, then you can add on, but most producers start with at least a guitar or piano, and add on from there.

## 52. *Try to add one of the following: mandolin, banjo, fiddle, steel guitar.*

As we said previously, these are just a few of the classic country instruments you should try to include in your recordings. If you listen back to more classic country songs, you will hear at least a few of these in almost every song. They might not all be in every song, but a few of them certainly will be. These are technically "accent instruments", meaning they are the next step after piano or guitar, but if you want to record a full-on, real-deal country song, you need at least a couple of these.

# Expert Q & A:

Q: How did you know when your production was "right"?

A: I think the first thing was that I have always been very conscious of never releasing or doing anything until it was totally and completely ready, because someone I really look up to in the industry told me that at a young age. And I'll be honest, it took me years to find the production that felt right for me. I tried a couple different producers first, and to be honest, I didn't quite know what I wanted to sound like yet, so it was impossible for me to tell them what I wanted to sound like. I went into it with a little bit too open of a mind, and I ended up not liking what we ended up with. However, after trying these first few producers, a friend and cowriter of mine who is also a producer offered to give my songs a shot. He knows me personally and who I want to be as an artist, so he knew what I wanted to sound like. He knocked it out of the park. It's hard to explain, but when I heard how he had produced my songs, it just felt like it made them even better than they were before. I think that's the mark of a good producer, to enhance your song. So it took some time, but I highly recommend taking that time to get it right before you release anything.

# Chapter 5: The Voice

If you want to be a country singer-songwriter, you have to be able to sing. The good news is, you don't have to be a natural-born incredible singer; you just have to be willing to work hard enough at it to be able to control your voice and work it properly.

## *Voice lessons help everyone – even good singers.*

### 53. *Even if you think you're the best singer in the world, you should still get voice lessons. Even the most famous singers have voice coaches!*

Did you know that even Reba, Chris Stapleton, Carrie Underwood, Dolly Parton, and more have voice coaches they often meet with weekly, sometimes before every show? That's right – they are some of the most naturally gifted singers in country music, and they still meet with a voice coach to help them with proper technique. Sure, you can have natural talent, but no one is born with natural technique. It's something you have to learn. So even if you were gifted with a naturally incredible voice, you should still find a good voice coach and start taking lessons. They help everyone!

## 54. _Voice lessons help you learn more than just singing: proper breathing, proper stance, proper control, and more._

The reason voice lessons are so helpful is that they teach technique. Voice technique covers a variety of topics, because there are so many different things involved, and the main one is control. You have to reign your voice in so that you can learn to hit the exact right notes at the exact right time. In addition, breathing is the first thing you'll learn in voice lessons, because if you don't have enough breath, your vocals will get choppy and you can easily get off beat. Your voice coach will teach you tips on how to breathe in ways that fill your lungs better and faster, and tips on how to stand in order for your vocal cords to work at their best. There are plenty of tips that only a voice coach can teach you, one-on-one, to fine-tune your own voice. So you should do your best to find one and get the help you need, no matter how good you are.

## 55. _Find a voice coach who has experience teaching country singers, not just singers in general – singing country music is a totally different skillset._

There are obviously a million different genres, and each one requires a slightly different skillset. So, it's important that you find a voice coach who has worked with country singers before, and not just singing in general. Country music requires some different phrasings, even a different accent, one that you have to slightly incorporate in your music, even if you don't necessarily talk in a country accent. So, you should find a voice coach who can cater to your specific genre, and make you sound like a country star – if you find the wrong voice coach, your voice might start to sound not as much like you want it.

## Choose the right songs for your voice.

### 56. <u>Just because a song sounds good with someone else singing it, doesn't mean it will sound good when you sing it.</u>

Sorry, not sorry. This isn't a bad thing. Each of us have our own unique voices. I don't sound like Carrie Underwood or Chris Stapleton and you probably don't either. And that's okay, because *you sound like you!* It sounds cheesy and cliché, but in the music world and country music world especially, you have to stand out to be successful. So don't try to sing in someone else's style; create your own style, and get good at it. Perfect certain skills – vibrato, certain pronunciations, certain phrasings. Decide what feels right and what feels like you, and do it. Don't ever change it. No matter how far you go, stay true to what feels like you, and stick to it – proudly.

## 57. _You sing the song – don't let the song sing you._

This rule applies in fashion too: "You wear the dress – don't let the dress wear you." What does this mean, exactly? It means you're in charge. It means you have control over the song, and the song doesn't have control over you. It means when you're singing the song, the song doesn't seem to be stressing you out with a million key changes and jumps from note to note and changes in rhythm non-stop. If you are singing the song, you have confidence and power over the song. You are showing that you know the song and each and every one of its ins and outs – you are not, on the other hand, terrified that you are about to miss a note or mess up the rhythm. This may sound strange, but it is a common problem among singers who choose a song that is too lofty for their personal capabilities. It is better to choose a song that you are overly capable of singing and add your own fancy flair to it than to choose a song that is out of your range of capabilities and to make it obvious that this is the case. Choose to sing songs that you are comfortable singing, and then add your own personal touch to them. The key here: you are in control, always.

# *Mean what you're singing.*

## 58. *If you're singing something you don't mean, listeners can tell.*

Country music is all about authenticity. If your music isn't authentic, your fans can tell immediately. This means one thing: sing things you mean! If you are singing a song that doesn't align with your virtues or values or personal mindset, it will show in your vocals, whether you think so or not. You cannot physically sound like you mean something if you don't actually mean it. So sing songs you mean! Write songs that say things you would say if you were having a normal conversation. Write songs that say things you believe in, agree with, and want to say to the world. Most importantly, just sing things you mean.

Now, remember, you don't always have to write or sing songs that you have lived personally 100%. You can sing about things you haven't personally lived through. However, if you do sing about those things you haven't technically experienced, it's very important to put yourself in that mindset and become the narrator of the song you are singing. That way, your listener will really believe you. What listeners want is to relate to whatever you're singing, and to feel like they aren't alone in their feelings. But if you are singing something that doesn't sound believable, they will just continue to feel more alone, and continue to feel like they are the only ones who have experienced whatever it is they're feeling. In addition, let's say it again: country music is all about authenticity. So if you are coming across as inauthentic, people will almost immediately write you off. Just be authentic – simple as that! Chances are, even if you haven't technically been in the exact shoes of the narrator from whose perspective you are singing, you have almost definitely felt at least some sort of the feeling they are feeling. Figure out exactly what that feeling is, channel it, and then let it come across in the song you are performing.

## 59. *In country music, emotion in singing is more important than technique.*

Country music is also all about emotion. It's about all kinds of emotions: if you're singing a breakup song, your emotion should be heartbroken. If you're singing a love song, your emotion should be sensitive, sweet, in love. If you're singing a song about going out to the bar and having a good time, your emotion should be fun, lighthearted, exciting. The first step is to analyze the song and decide what emotion you want to convey while singing it. The second step is executing this. This means you have to put yourself in the mindset of that emotion while you're singing the song in order to channel the feeling. You have to feel it! Technique is important in some genres, and it's important in country music, but not nearly as important as feeling the song and expressing the right emotion. Some of the best country songs showcase the singer experiencing a voice crack on the verge of tears, or a slightly off-key note because they are smiling too big about a fun song. These emotions are endearing to listeners and make them want to listen to you. It makes you feel like a friend to them. And who doesn't love that?

## 60. _Country songs tell stories. Tell the story as if you are in the middle of it, living it._

This might not make sense at first glance, but it is a huge principle in country music: even if you haven't lived the particular story you are singing about, you should still feel the song. That means you have to put yourself in the narrator's shoes. Some examples of this are early country songs – Reba's "Fancy" and "The Night the Lights Went Out in Georgia." Blake Shelton's "Ole Red". In these songs, the singers didn't always necessarily live the stories, but they put themselves in the shoes of the storyteller so much so that the listeners really and truly believe they have lived that story. This is a powerful thing, because remember how we talked about how country music is about telling stories? Well, it doesn't always have to be your own personal story. (Remember, you can tell your friends' stories, or stories you've heard on TV or in movies or in books!) This means you have freedom – freedom to tell any story you want, in any setting you want, from the point of view of any character you want. You can put yourself in that character's shoes, and if you do that, there's only one rule: mean what you're singing. Even if you haven't lived it, try to relate to the character you are essentially playing, and mean the words you are saying.

# Expert Q & A:

Q: How do you decide on the right songs to record and release?

A: This is a hard question, because sometimes there are songs that I really love personally but my friends and family/audience/professional team just don't love as much. That's always frustrating, but the fact of the matter is that if I've written a song, I never dislike it, so I am happy to release any of my songs. The truth about the music business is that it's just that: a business. So one of the best rules I've ever been taught about music in general is that the best song always wins. So if that means I have to not record a song that I love because other people don't love it, so be it – I might love it personally, but when it comes to making money, sometimes you have to hold back the song you love personally for a song that you AND other people love, for the sake of building a fanbase and, well, making money. Don't get me wrong, I am not saying and would never say to sell out and record music you don't like or that doesn't represent you and who you are. I'm just saying if it comes down to releasing a song that you love that other people don't seem to love, and releasing a song that you AND other people love... release the second. If you want to be a commercial country star, you've got to record and write music that commercial audiences like.

# Chapter 6: The Brand

What is a "brand", you might ask? Your brand is, essentially, everything about you. Your brand is you as a whole – your personality, your "vibe", what people think of when they think of you as an artist. Your brand can be certain colors you love, or a certain style (such as retro, hippie, extravagant, sparkly, girly, farmer, etc.) There are plenty of ways to define your brand; the key is sticking to it.

## *Your clothes represent your personality.*

### 61.  *Country music used to be just cowboy boots and belt buckles. If that's not you, don't wear it!*

There is a common misconception that country singers have to wear "country" clothes. In the older days of country music, sure, people wore big belt buckles and cowboy boots and cowboy hats, and even rhinestone suits and dresses. However, these are not necessarily important anymore – country singers can wear whatever they want and still be country! So if you aren't a cowboy boots/hat/belt buckle kind of person, the answer as simple: wear something else. Nobody will think you're "less country" for it!

## 62. Wear what you would normally wear. Country music is about authenticity.

The authenticity we've talked about through the entirety of this book apply to all of country music, and that includes your clothes. Your clothes say a lot about you – relaxed, hippie, whimsical, fun, flashy, exciting, laid-back... there are so many things they can say about you, so your clothes should tell a story too. And they should tell your true story, not the story of a character, because country stars are real people!

## 63. Tell a story not only with your songs, but with your clothes as well.

The story you should be telling is one about your life. If you are actually a farmer or a cowboy, you should wear your normal attire. If you're a tomboy, wear laid-back clothes. If you have a big personality, wear more flashy clothes. Whatever your story is, find a way to tell it in your clothes. The first thing people see when they look at you is your outer appearance, and like it or not, this is what first impressions are based on. So tell a good story with your clothes, and a story that goes along with your songs!

When you get dressed every morning, try to ask yourself what story you want to tell with your clothes. Ask yourself how you are feeling that day and what message you want to give to the world. You should stick to your brand, if possible, but it's totally okay to stray a little bit and stretch the boundaries of your brand when you feel like it. If you have a story you want to tell to the world that day, channel it, and decide which outfit in your closet best tells that story.

## Album covers/graphics represent your songs.

### 64. Every bit of your graphics matter: photos, fonts, colors, everything.

If you choose a font or color scheme or photo that looks unprofessional, it immediately makes you look unprofessional. You and your brand are one cohesive unit, and your brand includes EVERYTHING creative that you do – including everything down to the fonts you use. And these fonts, colors, and more should not just be used on your album, but also, try to use them on your social media graphics too. You can pick a few and use them interchangeably, so don't feel too confined, but you should try and keep them constant. It's a psychological thing – when someone sees a color or font that you use often, their brain is automatically reminded of you, and that's what you want. Because if people think about you, they will think about your songs.

## 65. Take photos that capture you in your natural form. Again, country music is all about authenticity.

Photoshoots can often feel uncomfortable when you're starting out. That's okay! It's that way for all of us. So first of all, you should find a photographer who makes you feel as comfortable as possible, to make it feel at least a little less awkward if you aren't used to taking solo photos. In addition, you should find a photographer who knows who you are and who you want to be as an artist – not someone who is going to force you into awkward photos that just aren't you. That means they won't make you take sexy, scandalous shots if that's not who you are, and they won't make you stand in a field of flowers if you're more country-pop, and they won't make you take non-smiling photos if you're a smiley kind of person. When your fans see your photos, they need to see you, and not someone else.

## 67. Take photos in outfits that represent you. Country music is not about costumes.

When you do a photoshoot, it's tempting to get all dressed up in nice clothes and do full hair and makeup and go all out. If this is your thing and you do this on a regular basis, then you should absolutely do it for your photoshoots! But if not, you should wear something you normally wear. If you're a blue jeans every day kind of person, don't wear a sparkly dress in a photoshoot. If you're the kind of guy who never

86

wears anything but jeans and a t-shirt, don't wear a cowboy hat and studded jeans. You don't ever have to be someone you're not in country music, and that means in music, life, and photos!

# *Social media is your best friend.*

## **68. In terms of building a following, the best way to do so is social media.**

In past years, it was incredibly hard to build a following without a record label. However, thanks to social media, you can build a huge following without even meeting with a single label. USE. THIS. TOOL. It is so important. As country artists, I know, it's hard, because a lot of us are not social media kind of people. But in this case, it's very important to further your career.

## **69. Use social media as a platform for getting personal, not for putting on a show.**

But don't worry – you don't have to use social media like you see a lot of other people using it, putting on a fake persona with lots of makeup and glamorous hotels and gourmet meals and beaches and world travels. Social media was intended for connection, not for fakeness. So use your social media to get personal with your fans! Talk to them! When you talk to your fans, you break down a barrier that makes them think you are higher-up than them, and you make them feel like you're a person too, which you are. (Side note: none of us are ever "higher-up" than anyone else. This is a mentality that, luckily, a lot of country artists don't have, but some people do, and no one likes a person who makes them feel inferior.)

## 70. Get your fans involved, with contests, merch sales, livestreams, etc.

So how do you get personal with your fans, you may ask? Get them involved! And there are plenty of ways to do this. You can do livestream videos, where your fans can comment in live time and ask you questions or make song requests. You can do question and answer sessions, and let them ask you anything they want about you or your life or upcoming music. Another great way is contests and giveaways, because who doesn't love a giveaway? You can giveaway something random, like a gift card, or you can give away your own merch. Both things work, but the key is to ask your followers to tag friends in the comments and/or share your post to their stories. This not only gets them involved, but it also builds your following when their friends follow you, and then those people's friends follow you, and so on.

Here's an example of a contest/giveaway you could do. Consider this a script for a video you could make telling your fans about the contest.

"Hey guys! Happy Friday! I wanted to announce something exciting today. Next Friday, I will be releasing my new single, _____. And I need your help getting it out there in the world! So, I will be giving away a $25 Amazon gift card and a free t-shirt, signed by me. If you enter the giveaway, you will be entered to win both, and I'll announce it on my page next Friday! All you have to do to enter is tag at least 3 friends in the comments, and your name will be put in the drawing. If you share this post to your story, you'll get a bonus entry, and if you share it in a profile post, you'll get a third entry. I would so appreciate your help getting this song heard. Thanks so much for your support, I love y'all!"

In addition, you can get them involved by asking them to send in something that will be a part of your project. Here's an example of something I did for a song I was releasing.

"Hey y'all! Happy Thanksgiving. So, next month, I will be releasing my new single, 'Nothing to See Here.' It's a song about small towns, about loving where you grew up and loving where you came from. And we want to make a video about small towns and hometowns and loving where you come from. So, we need your help. I've decided I want to include some of your hometowns as well. So, if you don't mind, I would love it if you could take a short, 10-second video of your hometown – it could be a certain place, like the movie theater or a drive thru or your high school or a football field. Or it could be your home, your street – whatever reminds you the most of home. When you send them in, we will incorporate them all into a video, and the video will show all of our hometowns together. So when you watch it, you can show all your hometown friends that your town is featured! I am so excited for y'all to hear this song, and I would really appreciate your help making this video and promoting this song. If you want to help, just DM me your video and it will definitely be included. Thank you so much!"

## 71. Show your personal life – country music fans want to know you are just like them!

There is definitely a line between sharing and oversharing, so share what you feel comfortable with. But country fans love to know that you are just like them. They respect it and are endeared by it. So show social media whatever you feel like is worth sharing that makes it clear you are a regular person – show them your family, or yourself going fishing, or when you just cleaned your truck, or you and your friends hanging out on your porch. Whatever makes it clear that you are a normal person! If it feels kind of boring, it might just be exactly what your fans need to see. Because sometimes, normal life is boring, but it's still worth sharing, because we all have normal lives, and it makes us feel connected. And that's what social media was intended for.

## Expert Q & A:

**Q:** How do you figure out what your brand is?

**A:** To be honest, I kind of don't love the idea of a brand, because I think people are so much more than that. But it's definitely a part of creating a successful career, so it's important. My best advice for finding out what your brand is, is just to make it, well, you! Decide on some things you love, things that you think sum you up as a person. Your brand colors are just your favorite colors, your fonts can be swirly and pretty or blocky and athletic-looking or faded and rustic, whatever you think fits your personality best. Your brand is basically a mixed-media self-portrait you are creating of yourself. So don't leave anything out that is pertinent to you and your personality! I think the worst thing you can possibly do when working on your brand is to try to make it something you're not. If you want to make your music career feel like a job, this is a surefire way to do it – you will constantly be feeling the need to keep up an act and maintain an image that just isn't you, and it will get exhausting. Find the things about your personality that you want to focus on and highlight, and make those your brand. Let's say it again, since we've said it so many times already, because it's that important: country music is all about authenticity. That means your brand is authentic and particular to you, not a character you are trying to play. Country music fans can smell fakeness a mile away.

# Chapter 7: The Performance

Your live show is SO important to your overall career. It is equally as, if not more, important than your recordings and production. Country music fans love to attend live shows to see their favorite stars live. But if you put on a boring or unorganized live show, they will immediately lose interest. That means your performance has to be top-notch, for every show – fully rehearsed and fully ready to control the stage and command the room.

## *Choose the right band for your music.*

### *72. Getting a band who represents your music well is just as important as a producer who represents your music well.*

A band represents and highlights your music just like a producer does, but your band just does it in a live setting instead of a recorded setting. This means they possibly have to be even better than your producer, because they don't have room to correct errors when onstage – they have to play properly all the time, whereas a producer can go back and correct errors. Find a band that represents you in the best possible light and adds to your music, doesn't take away from it. Find a band with people that are okay with being backup and supporting you, and not worried about stealing your spotlight, because this can cause for some arguments. Sometimes, band members are used to being solo artists, and it can be a hard adjustment from playing solo to playing in another artist's band. However, if you truly want to be a solo artist and one of your band members continuously gets jealous and tries to be center stage, it's very important to address this. This speaks to another fact in the music world, that you have to get very comfortable standing up for yourself and speaking your mind when you have something to say. Otherwise, you will get steamrolled over. In this case, you might end up in a duo with another person that you never intended to start, all because you had a lead guitar player who didn't like being backup and weaseled his way up to the front with you.

## 73. Find a band you get along well with – you will be spending a lot of time with them!

You will be spending SO much time with your band – perhaps more than with anyone else you work with. You will spend time with your band in the car, in the bus, on the road, onstage, in rehearsal, in hotels, and so much more. So you will inevitably get very close with them. And that means you need to get along with them, or else traveling and touring with them can become a terrible and stressful experience, really taking away from the overall enjoyment of your touring career. Find people that you want to hang out with, not just play music with. Find people you enjoy being around and people you agree on things with, such as music styles and overall values. You don't have to have best friends in your band, but you do need to have people you don't mind spending lots and lots of time with. So, choose them wisely.

## 74. You don't need to break the bank on a band.

Experienced band players can be very expensive. But don't worry! There is no rule that says you need band players with lots of experience when you start out, because when you're starting out, you don't have much experience either. So, you want to find people who are young and hungry and want to come up with you. You can all achieve your ultimate goal together, which is to make it in the business. And they will learn along the way just like you will. The good thing is, since they're just starting out too, they know you don't have a lot of money to spend on paying a band. That means they will be willing to not charge you too much and be willing to work hard to make tips for you all to split while playing.

## 75. Find bandmates who play real instruments, not DJs with track.

This one is pretty self-explanatory – you can always add a DJ or "track guy" to play some programmed tracks during your show, but start with the basics, then add on from there, if you want to!

# *Play for anyone who will listen.*

## *76. When you're starting out, you can't be picky about your venues.*

This is a BIG one. This is something that is hard to accept, but it is a real truth in the music world and in any business world: you have to start small. In the beginning stages, and really for a while after that, you have to play wherever anyone will listen to you. That means bars, clubs, Church, restaurants, patios, backyards, birthday parties, weddings, a street corner – wherever people will pay you a split second of attention, you should go there and play your songs. It can be hard and discouraging, but unless you are playing for literally zero people, you are making strides toward success. People who see you will tell their friends, and those friends will tell their friends, and before you know it, people will be flocking to your shows! But you have to start small.

## *77. If you want to play the big stages, you have to play the small stages first.*

So what are the small stages? This doesn't just mean the smaller scale stages at CMA Fest. No, this means as small as small can get. Like I said, it means street corners. It means if you have to play at your little cousin's birthday party, you should. It means if you have to ask a local restaurant owner if you can play on their patio on Tuesday nights, you should. It means if you get to play at a bar but there are only 2 people, in the crowd, you should. Here's the thing: nobody falls to the top. You have to push your way up. You have to pay your dues and work hard and put blood, sweat, and tears into it, and that means you're going to have to play some stages you most likely do not enjoy playing. But we all have to do it! And it makes your successes feel so much more worth it.

## 78. Play for free if you have to. You have to spend money to make money!

Most people are not willing to pay an artist much if they are just starting out, and sometimes, they aren't willing to pay you at all. Often, you are allowed to play for tips, and that is great! If you have a good enough set and engage with the crowd, you can make plenty of tips. If a booker says they cannot pay you, do not decline the offer – exposure is your payment. They are paying you by letting you play for a crowd, an opportunity that you most likely to not get often, and unless you have another offer for the same night that does pay, you should take the gig. If you have to spend a little money to pay your band or travel to the venue, try to make it work and spend the money, because you will eventually make it all back when you become a big success.

## 79. Country music is perfect for backyard barbecues, parties, and patios.

When it comes to starting out, country artists have a leg up over most other genres: country music is perfect to play acoustically, meaning all you need is a guitar and/or a cajon or tambourine if you want. So, you can pretty much play anywhere and everywhere with plenty of freedom. If you're struggling to find venues to play, throw a party and play in your backyard! Or ask a friend to throw a party. Or advertise to neighbors that you are available for hire for barbecues and other parties. When you do this, you are not only building your chops as a performer, but you are also making more friends. And friends can be fans too.

# Promote your shows well.

## 80. No one will come to your shows if they don't know they're happening.

When you're first starting out, there most likely are not people constantly checking your website for tour dates and places you're playing. That means you have to shout it from the rooftops every time you play a show, because if you don't, who's going to come to your show? Post about it on social media. Tell your friends. Post flyers around town. Do whatever it takes to make sure people know you are playing a show. And give them reasons they should attend even more than just the fact that you're playing! Tell them you'll be buying the first 10 people drinks, or you'll be giving away free shirts, or just that the bar has great food that they don't want to miss. Don't ever make empty promises, because that's a surefire way to get people not to come to another of your shows. Instead, stick to your word, and also, the most important part: put on a good show.

## 81. Promote your shows with family and friends first versus random places – country music is built on grassroots movements.

If you don't have a big social media following yet, don't worry! Country music was built on grassroots movements: people helping each other simply by banding together and helping each other out by word of mouth. So, tell everyone you know. If you're playing a big show, send an email to everyone who has ever supported your music in your whole time playing. Text your friends – personally, not in a group text, so that they know you thought of them individually and wanted to reach out to them because you know they believe in you. Group chats and snapchats can come across as impersonal, because you can send them to whoever. Send personal messages and tell people how much it would mean to you if they would come to your show. It will not only build your fanbase, but also spark some better connections with old friends – people love to feel like they are a part of your journey, and by asking them to come to your shows, you are inviting them into this journey.

## Expert Q & A

**Q.** What are some small things you can add to a live show that make a big difference?

**A.** There are two seemingly small things that you can add into your live show that I think make a big difference, because when I started incorporating them, it changed the whole dynamic of my show. The first is called "moveable focus", and it's a trick my voice coach taught me about how to connect with the audience without staring anyone straight in the eyes and making them feel uncomfortable. Moveable focus is basically the concept of looking in a general direction or at the top of a certain person's head for 5-10 seconds, then moving or shifting your focus to another spot of top of another person's head, then moving again. It's important to look at the top of their head and not straight in the eyes because psychology shows that this makes people uncomfortable if they don't know you personally. But by moving and shifting your focus while singing, you make sure to give the entire crowd your attention, and everyone knows you are thankful they are there.

The second thing I started doing was literally involving the crowd in my show. This is something you should ask the venue about for each show, but it's great at birthday and backyard parties, as well as venues where the owner is comfortable. Basically, the only thing you do is bring up one or two people to sing a song or two with you during your show. If you see some little kids singing along, invite them up! If there are some teenage girls who know every word, invite them! If you're singing at a birthday party, by all means, invite the birthday boy/girl. Inviting this person up onstage not only gets them involved, but all their friends as well. And if you can get the crowd involved and invested in your show, then you will not only win them over, but you'll have a great time.

# Chapter 8: The Business

Ahh, the business – yes, it's not quite as fun as the creative side of things. But if you want to be successful and have a career doing music, you simply have to establish yourself in the business side of music, and not just the fun parts. The music business requires hard work, and that means it requires learning more about the business side of things than you might like. Ultimately, it will help you tremendously in your career and overall success.

## *Meet with publishers.*

### 82. You don't need a publisher, but they really, really help.

For those of you who don't know, let's talk about publishers for a minute. What do they do exactly? We've already talked about producers, and producers and publishers also get confused because of their similar letters – however, these are two very different things. Let's start with this: publishers deal with songwriters. Songwriting is the focus of publishers. What a publisher does is take your song, listen to it and decide if they like it or what you could possibly change about it, then get back to you. Then, if they like it, they will send it/show it, or "pitch" it, to any country music artist who is "cutting" songs at the moment. "Cutting" is another songwriting term, and it sounds like a bad thing, but it's actually the opposite: when someone wants to cut your song, it means they want to put it on their album. For instance, sometimes, when I walk into a cowriting session, someone will say, "Blake Shelton is cutting right now, should we try to write for him today?" They keyword is "try", because your song only gets cut if the artist and their team like it. But essentially, a publisher's job is to get your songs heard and cut by bigger artists. If you want to sing your own songs, even better – you are the one cutting your own songs, so the publisher's job is to then set you up with other cowriters so that you can continue writing good songs. Publishers pay you a monthly salary if you sign a publishing deal with them, and then, if you get a song cut or a song of yours starts making money, they make a small percentage.

The reason publishers aren't totally necessary is because you can technically find cowriters on your own, and you can technically pitch songs to artists on your own. However, this is incredibly hard, because artists and their teams are far more likely to listen to a song sent from a well renowned publisher than from a random stranger in their email inbox. So, a publisher is extremely helpful and more likely to get your songs heard.

## 83. Play them your best songs, even if you're tired of them.

If you want to sign a publishing deal, you should definitely show the publishing company your very best songs. There's a songwriting rule that everyone's favorite song they've written is the latest song they've written. Don't let this rule get in your head when you meet with a publisher – if you do, you might end up playing a new song you love but that you won't love in a couple weeks, and then you'll regret that that was their first and sometimes only impression of you. Instead, play your tried and true songs, the ones your family and friends and even audiences like if you've played it live. It doesn't matter how tired you are of playing them – remember, it's their first time hearing it, so they want to hear the best you've got.

# *Meet with record labels.*

## *84. You don't need a record label. But they really, really help.*

As we just discussed, you can build a perfectly big following without an ounce of record label help. However, there are certain things record labels do that you simply can't do on your own, unless you have buckets and buckets of money. First, let's talk about what a record label does. People often get confused on the difference between record deals and publishing deals, so right here is your answer: plain and simple, publishing companies work with songwriters, and record labels work with performers/artists. So, ideally, when you reach a high point in your career, you will have both, because they work with separate parts of the industry.

But for now, let's talk about record labels. What do they do? Record labels do a lot of things. For starters, they pay for a lot of things for you that would normally cost a fortune. Technically, you pay them back a percentage of your earnings, but it's still just a percentage. Record labels pay for recordings, promotion, tour, photoshoots, even clothes for shows sometimes. They also use their connections to boost your career in the eyes of the industry, meaning they spread the word about you to other industry executives, making your name popular in Nashville – this is incredibly important if you are up-and-coming. There are pros and cons to major labels and pros and cons to smaller ones, but the ultimate rule is to analyze the companies individually and decide which you like best. If they want you and you want them, you've got a perfect match. But wait for that perfect match, because signing a deal is a big deal (no pun intended), and it's something that requires a lot of thought and hard work. That said – don't worry about it quite yet, because starting out, you really don't need a record deal. So take a deep breath – we're just going to get you ready for the day when you are ready for one.

## **85. Go to your meetings as if you are playing a show, dressed like an artist.**

It's tempting to show your confidence by walking in in casual clothes, showing them that you do this every day and you are used to playing for people. However, the fact of the matter is that most labels know they are a coveted, important phenomena in Nashville, so they know you have been very excited for this meeting, because frankly, their time is valuable. By showing up totally and completely ready to "wow" them, you show them that you respect the fact that they are giving you their time, and that you appreciate that they want to listen to you. In addition, you should ALWAYS be on time. There is no better way to show someone you don't care about their time than to show up late.

## 86. Always bring your guitar.

Going along with this, you should always be prepared. That means bring your guitar, to pretty much any music meeting you go to. Sometimes they won't, but most times, they will want to hear a song or two played live, especially at a record label meeting. How you perform live is incredibly important, both in front of the crowd, but also, in a small office-style room with just a few people, because radio tour is exactly that: playing for a few people in a small office-style room. They want to see that you have a gift, that you can play at the drop of a hat. In addition, it shows that you are always prepared.

## 87. Be nice to people. Nobody wants to work with someone who is rude.

This one is one of the most important things to learn in any industry. Just be nice. It sounds simple, but somehow, so many people don't do it. Being nice is simply a way to sleep better at night, because obviously, doing the right thing is the best way to get through life. But it will get you through the music business too. There is an arrogance complex that many people think comes along with becoming an artist. But this is not true – no one want to work with someone who is arrogant and rude. In fact, there are many artists who have lost record deals and publishing deals simply because they were rude people. So don't be that person. Just be nice. It's not that hard.

## *Work with people who care about the music more than the money.*

### 88. Work with people who remind you why you started: for the music, not for the money.

There are tons of people in the music business. Luckily, country music is notorious for having lots of good, down-to-earth people in the environment, but still, there are bad seeds everywhere. That means you have to find the good ones and work with them, and if someone strikes you as a bad seed, have the courage to walk away. There are plenty of people in this business for the money, as there are in other businesses as well. To them, you are a pawn, a tool for them to use to make money. They do not see you as a person, but rather, a product to market. Steer clear of these people. Whatever you do, do not give these people your time and energy, because you are worth more.

Work with people who love country music, who know the classics and have posters on their office wall of Hank Williams, Jr. and George Jones. When you work with people who truly appreciate the music and are in it for that, first and foremost, your work life will have so much more purpose. You will feel so at home with your team, and you will feel so understood – like they really are in it for the music, and not just to make money off you.


## 89. Work with people you enjoy working with – you'll be seeing a lot of them.

There are two different kinds of relationships in the music world: your creative relationships, and your business relationships. We have talked about the creative ones – cowriters, producers, band members, etc. But now, we're going to talk about the business ones, which are equally as important. Your creative relationships are the ones that control the creative, "fun" side of your career, while your business relationships are the relationships that control the technical and logistical aspects of your career. I know, it's not as fun, but it's important, so if you end up with people you don't like, you'll end up with people you are always at odds with, and this is a recipe for disaster. That means you should take seriously the people you are working with, and not just go with the first person who offers you a deal – you should enjoy working with them. In the country world, people all hang out together often, and work relationships are usually more than just that. So, if you want to build a work relationship with them, make sure you could build a friendship with them too.

## 90. Work ethic is more important than talent. Work hard. (Plus, country music listeners are hard-working people.)

This one sounds so simple, but it is not. So many people think they will just float on up to the top because they have natural talent. But these are the people that will sink, almost immediately. If you don't put in the work, you don't get the reward. In fact, I've heard it said that succeeding in the music industry is 30% talent and 70% work ethic. I would agree with this completely. You can be the most talented singer in the world, but if you don't work hard to achieve your goals, you simply will not achieve them. They say Nashville is a 10-year town, meaning it takes 10 years to really make it in the industry. Don't let this discourage you: country music listeners love and respect a hard-working person, because most of them are hard-working folks themselves. The country music audience are small-town, good American people, and they respect and appreciate hard work. You should too. If it takes hard work, it shouldn't matter, because if you love it enough, you would work for it forever. So, work for it. It'll pay off.

## 91. Find a manager who believes in you.

Perhaps the most important business relationship you will have is with your manager. Your manager does a million and one things to help you in your career. You won't need a manager until you get a little further into your career, but when you do find that it is the time to hire one, be as picky as you need. Find someone you get along with and enjoy spending time with, just like anything else. But more than anything, the most important thing to look for in a manager is that they believe in you, fully and wholeheartedly. Finding someone who believes in you is something you simply cannot buy. If they believe in you, they will fight for you, they will promote you, they will do whatever it takes to make sure you achieve all of your goals. And this is what you need. You need as many people like this on your team as possible. If they don't believe in you, you won't be a priority to them, and you deserve to be a priority. So find someone who makes you one.

## 92. *Find a booking agency that believes in you.*

Another important part of your business team is your booking agency. What does a booking agency do exactly? Put simply, they book shows for you. They also book meet-and-greets, travels, plane tickets, all of it – once you get to a certain level, they book and schedule every performance for you that you need. But this one goes with the manager one. They are a very important relationship, and you will be working with and seeing and talking to these people often. So, you need to make sure they really and truly believe in you. If they don't, they usually have lots of other clients, and you will not be a priority to them. That means you should not stay with them if they don't believe in you. You can always find someone else.

## 93. If you need to walk away from people who aren't a good fit, do it.

This is a hard one. Finding a good business team is hard, so even if you find people who aren't all that great, you feel tempted to stick with them, because as I said, they can be hard to find. I encourage you to be brave enough to walk away if they aren't right for you. This is your dream, your love, your favorite thing to do in the whole world. And while it will definitely feel like a job sometimes, because it is, it should not grow to be something you dread. And if you are working with people who make you dread doing this, you should simply not be working with them. It doesn't have to be a big break-up – it can just be a simple, "I don't think we are a great fit working together." And leave it at that. Your life is too short to work with people who aren't right for you to work with. And you will find the right people.

## Expert Q & A:

**Q:** How do you break into the business and meet people in the industry?

**A:** We've all heard the saying, "It's not what you know, it's who you know." This is true in every industry, including country music. Fortunately, Nashville has a reputation for being a warm and welcoming town, and this reputation is certainly accurate. People are typically very supportive and helpful to up-and-coming artists and want to help. That means you just have to meet them! Making connections in Nashville is not nearly as hard as it seems – it can feel daunting and nerve wracking at first, but it's really not that bad. You just have to see and be seen. That means go to shows, big and small – arena shows and little bar shows and coffee shop shows, where you can meet and associate with your peers in the industry. The more friends you make, the more connections you make, and someone always knows someone who knows someone who can help further your career. The trick is to really make genuine and authentic friendships instead of always trying to network – number one, it's exhausting to always be in work mode, and number two, this business can be hard, so you need a support system of music peers who know what it's like. In addition to making these friendships, if you ever meet an industry professional, don't hesitate to ask to take them to coffee to pick their brain. Never approach it in a way that says, "I want to show you some of my songs and get a record deal!" because this can come across as too forward and a bit selfish. However, if you go into it with the sole intention of asking their advice and getting some mentorship from them on how to further your career, this will build a relationship that will definitely help you further down the line – even if it's just that they know your name and that you're a good person, which will make it so that they speak highly of you. Don't rush it – just go out there and try to meet people, and the big connections will come. In summary, I guess the place to start is just to make friends in the industry.

# Chapter 9: The Person (You!)

This is the most important chapter, so we've saved the best for last. This whole thing is about YOU. The music business is a hard one, because in most businesses, you are selling, advertising for, promoting, and working for a certain product. But in this case, the product is you and your music. So it can feel very personal. This means you have to take all necessary measures to protect and take care of yourself. You have to do everything that needs to be done to make sure you are functioning at your best, and most importantly, that you are healthy and happy and not working yourself too hard.

## *First and foremost, you are a human.*

### **94. Before you are an artist, writer, or performer, you are human. That means you don't have to be perfect!**

This is SUCH an important one. My publisher told me when she signed me something that will stick with me forever. She said, "I want you to know that yes, your career is songwriting, but that's not who you are. You are a human, and a human first. So whatever you need to do to be a healthy human, by all means, that always comes first." That was one of the most important and profound things anyone has said to me for my entire career. Because it's so easy to make our job our identity. Think about it: when someone asks you about yourself, the first thing we almost always say is our job. It's not a bad thing – our jobs take up a lot of our time. But this job is not your identity. You are a person, a human being, and that means your job comes second. Your job comes second to family, to home life, to your own personal wellbeing. Never forget that. It's a hard lesson to accept when you know how hard you have to work at achieving this dream, but at the end of the day, your job is not the most important thing in your life. Even if this is your dream and you would do it without making a single dime (which most of us would), you still have to live your life and take care of yourself.

## 95. Live your life. Not for the purpose of being a good artist, but just for the purpose of living a good life.

When you decide you want to become a country music singer-songwriter, you decide you want to devote all your time and energy to that. And suddenly, every single thing you do revolves around that, and you have no free time anymore, and you live and breathe music business. For some people, this is great – and in fact, it's okay to live and breathe music. But it's incredibly unhealthy to live and breathe music business. This leaves you in a constant state of stress and trying to climb the ladder, so much so that you miss out on the rest of your life and enjoying quality time with your friends and family. It's so important to create balance here. It's so important to make sure you are not spreading yourself too thin in the work world and that you still have time for your own health and wellbeing at the end of the day. You have to live your life. Go on trips, go to parties, have friends over for dinner, cook delicious meals. Sure, all of these things can spark song ideas, but you shouldn't do them just for that purpose – you should do them for the sole purpose of loving and taking care of yourself. That is the most important thing, and the song ideas just come as a biproduct.

## 96. Stay true to yourself. Don't do anything that makes you feel uncomfortable or unsafe.

Let me get real with you for just a second. In the music business, and many businesses, there are certain executives who will pressure you into doing things you are not comfortable with in exchange for helping make you successful. We would hope the country music world would be immune to this, but like any industry, there are nasty and awful people in every single job you could ever do. That means you have to watch out. People will promise you all kinds of wonderful things that you will get as long as you do certain things for them. But this is never the answer. So many people fall prey to this, and I encourage you to not, under any circumstances, let it be you. It doesn't matter what they promise or what they offer or what they threaten you with if you are unwilling. Have the courage to walk away. Your discomfort and going against your morals and values is never worth any level of success. And if you feel unsafe, immediately, walk away. That is your answer right there – if you feel uncomfortable or unsafe, it's time to go. Get out, and never look back. You will never regret it.

## 97. Don't let anyone change you.

Even if people aren't harming you dangerously mentally or physically, people will still try to change you in the music industry. As I said, it applies in other industries, but it also applies in the country music industry, unfortunately – it's just how the music business goes in general sometimes. But that doesn't mean you have to go along with it. We are all so afraid of hurting someone's feelings that we will do whatever they say, even if we don't agree with it.

# Put your mental health first.

## 98. Mental health comes before any work project.

Mental health is far more important than most people give it the attention for. If your career requires you to jeopardize your mental health, you should change something about it. If you are working too hard on your music and it begins to mess up your mental health, it will only get worse. A music career can be a stressful one, with little sleep, many hours on the road, and your whole life being watched and doted on by other people. If you realize you are getting too stressed, take a step back, analyze some things, and take a break if you need to. Your mental health comes first, always, so if it begins to decline, don't be afraid to slow down.

In addition, if your music career begins to ramp up, consider getting therapy, even just as a preventative measure. Many creative people in general suffer from anxiety, depression, and other mental health disorders, simply because our brains are overactive and we think about things very deeply. It's not something to be embarrassed of or worried about – it's something to be proud of if you are willing to put your mental health first and take matters into your own hands by taking care of yourself.

## 99. Physical health is important too.

Physical health and mental health are both important. And I want you to notice something – that does not say "thinness" or "skinniness" is important. It says physical health. Physical health and these two things can be very different. In the music industry and any industry in which you are in the public eye, it can be very easy to fall into the trap that says you have to be skinny, even if it requires you to achieve this in unhealthy ways. But let me tell you, if anyone ever asks you to jeopardize your own health in order to look a certain way, they are not meant to be on your team – nothing is worth risking your own personal mental and physical health.

Physical health is so important because it makes you feel good. If you feel bad or feel bad about yourself, you won't be able to perform well in any setting, in work or life in general. Exercise gives you endorphins, a chemical that makes you happy. And eating right gives your body the energy it needs to function properly and at its highest level.

All of this said, I highly encourage you to not get sucked into the mindset that says you have to be skinny, whatever it takes. This is not true. There are people who are succeeding tremendously in the country music industry who do not fit the Hollywood standard for beauty, and they are equally as beautiful and talented and successful. Follow in their footsteps. Do what is healthy for your body, not what you feel like you have to do according to what the world says you have to be or look like. This is a dangerous game to play, and it can result in serious health risks. And nothing, no career, no dream is worth risking your own wellbeing. Be wary of it, watch out for it, and don't let it happen to you. If it does, have the courage to notice it, call it out, and make a change, whether that means in your team or just in your own personal mindset and actions.

## 100. If it doesn't make you happy, it might not be the right thing for you. And that's okay.

Why did you start making music in the first place? Because it makes you happy, right? I'm assuming the answer is yes. If you ever start to feel unhappy doing it, think about this long and hard, because this is a career you have to fully dedicate yourself to – not just do for fun, if you really want to succeed. So, here are a few questions to ask yourself when deciding whether or not you really want to do this and be a full-time country music singer-songwriter.

- Do I want to do this for the rest of my life?
- Would I do this if I never made a single dime doing it?
- Do I love this with my whole entire heart?
- Do I love country music, not just music in general?
- Do I love being onstage and playing for a crowd?
- Do I love writing songs?
- Do I love writing songs with other people?
- Do I love listening to country music that my friends and peers make?
- Am I willing to spend some money before I make any money?
- Am I willing to work as hard as I need to to make my dream a reality?
- Do I want this with everything I have?

If you are hesitant on any one of these questions, this might not be the career for you. And you know what? That's okay! However, if you feel certain this is what you want to do, do it with your whole heart. If it starts to feel too much like a job, do something that reminds you why you love it – listen to your favorite artist's album or go to a show or write a song by yourself, the way you started out. It's going to feel like a job sometimes, because it is one, and that's normal. There is nothing you can ever do that is worthwhile that doesn't require hard work, discipline, and a little bit of nose-to-the-grindstone dirty work and elbow grease. However, it will always be worth it. Remind yourself why it makes you happy and why you love it. Always, always, always remind yourself why you started, and this will continuously propel you to the top.


# *Have fun!*

## *101. ENJOY THE RIDE.*

As with any career, becoming the next country music superstar is not an easy road. You will encounter many roadblocks, many bumps in the road, many times you think you want to turn around completely. And it's easy to get caught up on the destination. But it's important to focus on the journey. Some of the best memories you will make as an up-and-coming musician are the things you do on your way to the top. You will stay in rundown hotels and take turns with your bandmembers sleeping on the floor. Your rental car will break down and you will barely make it to your own show. You will forget your guitar and have to use the bartender's, who happens to play music on the side and keeps his guitar in the green room. You will make friends and meet hilarious people and see wild and beautiful places. Some days you will leave the writing room with a song you hate, and some days you will leave the writing room with a song that makes you remember why you even like music in the first place.

# *Expert Q & A:*

Q: What made you get into country music in the first place?

A: I got into country music, first and foremost, because I was just a fan. I grew up listening to country music, and I loved all the songs I grew up listening to, I just thought, "Wow, I want to create songs like that." I also loved to write stories and sing, so it just felt natural to get into the business, and that's why I started so young.

I love country music for so many reasons: I love the people, the fans, the writers and artists. Everyone is so genuine, just down-to-earth, good, kindhearted, hardworking people, and it's hard to find such a large community of people like this. I love getting to walk into a room with people I love and talk about our lives and write a song about it. I love hearing a crowd sing the words I wrote back to me. I love standing in a crowd and singing another artist's words back to them. Honestly, to me, country music just feels like home.

# Conclusion

So, I know – it's a lot! But if you love it, it's worth it. If you love country music and want to make it as a successful country singer-songwriter, you can absolutely do it if you work hard enough. Garth Brooks was told "no" by almost 10 record labels before one finally said yes and he blew up to be one of the biggest country stars of all time. So if you get a few doors slammed in your face, don't give up! The country music business is a special place to be, and I am thankful to be lucky enough to work in such a special industry. Good luck, keep making music, and keep having fun!

# About the Expert

Caroline Watkins has lived and breathed country music since the day she was born. Born and raised in Nashville, TN, she started writing songs as soon as she could read, and began performing around Nashville at the young age of 13. At 17, she was given the opportunity to play her own songwriters' round at the legendary Bluebird Café, Nashville's top songwriting venue, and has been a regular there ever since.

The day before her high school graduation, Watkins signed a worldwide publishing deal with Warner-Chappell Music Publishing, where she is still signed as a songwriter to this day. Since then, she has opened for country stars such as Brett Eldredge, Walker Hayes, and the legendary Willie Nelson.

Watkins continues to perform all over the country with her band and to write songs with Grammy-winning country songwriters on a daily basis. She loves country music and being a part of the country music family.

HowExpert publishes quick 'how to' guides on all topics from A to Z by everyday experts. Visit HowExpert.com to learn more.

# Recommended Resources

- HowExpert.com – Quick 'How To' Guides on All Topics from A to Z by Everyday Experts.
- HowExpert.com/free – Free HowExpert Email Newsletter.
- HowExpert.com/books – HowExpert Books
- HowExpert.com/courses – HowExpert Courses
- HowExpert.com/clothing – HowExpert Clothing
- HowExpert.com/membership – HowExpert Membership Site
- HowExpert.com/affiliates – HowExpert Affiliate Program
- HowExpert.com/writers – Write About Your #1 Passion/Knowledge/Expertise & Become a HowExpert Author.
- HowExpert.com/resources – Additional HowExpert Recommended Resources
- YouTube.com/HowExpert – Subscribe to HowExpert YouTube.
- Instagram.com/HowExpert – Follow HowExpert on Instagram.
- Facebook.com/HowExpert – Follow HowExpert on Facebook.

Made in the USA
Las Vegas, NV
17 January 2024